SHEPHERD'S NOTES

SHEPHERD'S NOTES

When you need a guide through the Scriptures

Jeremiah/ Lamentations

BROADMAN
&HOLMAN
PUBLISHERS

Nashville, Tennessee

Shepherds Notes®—*Jeremiah-Lamentations*
© 1998 Broadman & Holman Publishers, Nashville, Tennessee
All rights reserved
Printed in the United States of America

ISBN# 0-8054-9070-1

Dewey Decimal Classification: 224.20
Subject Heading: BIBLE. O.T. JEREMIAH
Library of Congress Card Catalog Number: 98-48096

Library of Congress Cataloging-in-Publication Data

House, Paul R., 1958–
      Jeremiah & Lamentations / Paul House., editor [i.e. author].
         p.   cm. — (Shepherd's notes)
      Includes bibliographical references.
      ISBN 0-8054-9070-1 (trade paper.)
      1. Bible.   O.T.   Jeremiah—Study and teaching. 2 Bible. O.T.
Lamentations—Study and teaching   I. Title.   II. Title: Jeremiah and
Lamentations. III. Series.
BS1525.5.H68   1999   98-48096
224'.207—dc21   CIP

1 2 3 4 5 6   03 02 01 00 99 98

CONTENTS

Dear Reader:

Shepherd's Notes are designed to give you a quick, step-by-step overview of every book of the Bible. They are not meant to be substitutes for the biblical text; rather, they are study guides intended to help you explore the wisdom of Scripture in personal or group study and to apply that wisdom successfully in your own life.

Shepherd's Notes guide you through the main themes of each book of the Bible and illuminate fascinating details through appropriate commentary and reference notes. Historical and cultural background information brings the Bible into sharper focus.

Six different icons, used throughout the series, call your attention to historical-cultural information, Old Testament and New Testament references, word pictures, unit summaries, and personal application for everyday life.

Whether you are a novice or a veteran at Bible study, I believe you will find *Shepherd's Notes* a resource that will take you to a new level in your mining and applying the riches of Scripture.

In Him,

David R. Shepherd
Editor-in-Chief

DESIGNED FOR THE BUSY USER

Shepherd's Notes for Jeremiah and Lamentations is designed to provide an easy-to-use tool for getting a quick handle on these significant
Bible books, important features, and for gaining an understanding of
their messages. Information available in more difficult-to-use reference works has been incorporated into the *Shepherd's Notes* format.
This brings you the benefits of many advanced and expensive works
packed into one small volume.

Shepherd's Notes are for laymen, pastors, teachers, small-group leaders
and participants, as well as the classroom student. Enrich your personal study or quiet time. Shorten your class or small-group preparation time as you gain valuable insights into the truths of God's Word
that you can pass along to your students or group members.

DESIGNED FOR QUICK ACCESS

Bible students with time constraints will especially appreciate the
timesaving features built into the *Shepherd's Notes*. All features are
intended to aid a quick and concise encounter with the heart of the
messages of Jeremiah and Lamentations.

Concise Commentary. Short sections provide quick "snapshots" of the
themes of these books, highlighting important points and other
information.

Outlined Text. Comprehensive outlines cover the entire text of Jeremiah
and Lamentations. This is a valuable feature for following each book's
flow, allowing for a quick, easy way to locate a particular passage.

Shepherd's Notes. These summary statements or capsule thoughts
appear at the close of every key section of the narratives. While func-
tioning in part as a quick summary, they also deliver the essence of
the message presented in the sections which they cover.

Icons. Various icons in the margin highlight recurring themes in the books of Jeremiah and Lamentations, aiding in selective searching or tracing of those themes.

Sidebars and Charts. These specially selected features provide additional background information to your study or preparation. Charts offer a quick overview of important subjects. Sidebars include definitions as well as cultural, historical, and biblical insights.

Questions to Guide Your Study. These thought-provoking questions and discussion starters are designed to encourage interaction with the truth and principles of God's Word.

DESIGNED TO WORK FOR YOU

Personal Study. Using the *Shepherd's Notes* with a passage of Scripture can enlighten your study and take it to a new level. At your fingertips is information that would require searching several volumes to find. In addition, many points of application occur throughout the volume, contributing to personal growth.

Teaching. Outlines frame the text of Jeremiah and Lamentations, providing a logical presentation of their messages. Capsule thoughts designated as "Shepherd's Notes" provide summary statements for presenting the essence of key points and events. Application icons point out personal application of the messages of the books. Historical Context icons indicate where cultural and historical background information is supplied.

Group Study. *Shepherd's Notes* can be an excellent companion volume to use for gaining a quick but accurate understanding of the messages of Jeremiah and Lamentations. Each group member can benefit from having his or her own copy. The *Note's* format accommodates the study of themes throughout Jeremiah and Lamentations. Leaders may use its flexible features to prepare for group sessions or use them during group sessions. Questions to Guide Your Study can spark the discussion of Jeremiah and Lamentations's key points and truths to be discovered in these profound books.

LIST OF MARGIN ICONS USED IN JEREMIAH AND LAMENTATIONS

Shepherd's Notes. Placed at the end of each section, a capsule statement provides the reader with the essence of the message of that section.

Historical Context. To indicate historical information—historical, biographical, cultural—and provide insight on the understanding or interpretation of a passage.

Old Testament Reference. Used when the writer refers to Old Testament passages or when Old Testament passages illuminate a text.

New Testament Reference. Used when the writer refers to New Testament passages that are either fulfilled prophecy, an antitype of an Old Testament type, or a New Testament text which in some other way illuminates the passages under discussion.

Personal Application. Used when the text provides a personal or universal application of truth.

Word Picture. Indicates that the meaning of a specific word or phrase is illustrated so as to shed light on it.

Taken from Jeremiah/Lamentation, vol. 16, *New American Commentary* (Nashville, Tenn.: Broadman & Holman Publishers, 1993), p. 45.

INTRODUCTION

Few biblical books are as challenging to readers as Jeremiah. It does not unfold in chronological order, nor does it typically present an upbeat message. Set in the most turbulent era in Israelite history, it focuses upon the consequences of the chosen people's chronic rebellion against God. Without question, Jeremiah is a sad book that forces its readers to think. At the same time, Jeremiah includes some of the most hopeful promises in the Bible. Better days are ahead for believers, because a Savior is coming, a New Covenant will be made, and a more committed holy community will be formed. Therefore, it is important to read Jeremiah with hope, for there is always hope for those who serve God faithfully.

"All scripture is given by inspiration of God, and is profitable for doctrine, for reproof, for correction, for instruction in righteousness: That the man of God may be perfect, thoroughly furnished unto all good works" (2 Tim. 3:16, 17, KJV).

Reading Jeremiah is a grand adventure. Those who take its warnings seriously can avoid costly sins and grave errors in judgment. Those who identify with Jeremiah's pain will find strength for their own Christian service. Those who understand the book's emphasis on the New Covenant will have hope grounded in sound biblical theology. The effort expended to interpret this prophecy is well worth it. Jeremiah's message can still transform lives.

HISTORICAL SETTING

Jeremiah served as a prophet during an extraordinarily difficult era in Israelite history. At its conclusion, the last remnant of what had been David and Solomon's twelve-tribe kingdom perished. Several factors contributed to Judah's destruction, and Jeremiah preached about all of them.

During this period (627–587 B.C.) Judah was plagued by spiritual decline, failing leadership, and international imperialism. Several other prophets' ministries overlapped with Jeremiah's. Nahum, Habakkuk, and Zephaniah preached before the Exile, while Ezekiel prophesied mostly after the Exile. God used these prophets to warn Israel to repent before it was too late.

First, the nation suffered from a leadership vacuum brought about by constant change after Josiah's death. As 2 Kings 22:1–23:30 points out, Josiah was a king who served the Lord wholeheartedly during his reign (640–609 B.C.). During Josiah's monarchy Jeremiah was called to be a prophet in 627 B.C. (1:1–3). Five years later in 622 B.C., the king led a reform of Judah's religion after a copy of the Law of Moses was discovered in the Temple (2 Kings 23:1–25). This revival meant that the people at least had to pay lip service to biblical faith, but nothing in Jeremiah indicates it was deep-seated or particularly heartfelt.

When Josiah was killed in 609 B.C. by the Egyptian army, the reform died with him.

After Josiah's death his son Jehoahaz ruled for only three months (2 Kings 23:31). He did not please the Egyptians, who now called the political shots in Judah. Thus, they placed the compliant Jehoiakim on the throne, and he remained in power from 609 to 598 B.C. Jeremiah particularly detested this king (23:18–23), and Jehoiakim had no appreciation for the prophet's message (36:1–26). Jehoiakim was so politically pliable that he managed to switch loyalties from Egypt to Babylon in 605 B.C. so he could remain in power. Clearly, his main priority was self-preservation, not serving the people.

Jehoiakim was succeeded by Jehoiachin, who reigned for only three months during 598–597 B.C. Apparently he did not please the Babylonians, so they deposed him in favor of Zedekiah, Judah's final monarch (597–587 B.C.). A weak, vacillating ruler, Zedekiah sought Jeremiah's advice on many occasions, yet never followed his counsel. Eventually he opposed the Babylonians, so they conquered Jerusalem. Without question, every king who followed Josiah failed the Lord, which means they failed their people as well.

Second, Judah's inadequate leadership was in part produced by international imperialism. Egypt and Babylon dictated the direction of Judah's government. Babylon was the greatest threat, of course, since they backed demands with a mobile and destructive army. Jeremiah preached that Babylon was God's instrument for punishing wicked nations, and he also stated that Babylon would eventually be judged for wrongdoing (25:1–18). Judah rejected this message.

Third, the unstable political situation led to economic and social decline. Citizens sinned against one another through murder, theft, etc. (7:1–15). Jews held fellow Jews in servile bondage (34:8–22). Royalty used forced status to hoard wealth (22:13–17). The social fabric of the nation came unraveled as God's law was rejected.

Fourth, Judah's spiritual life deteriorated as well. Indeed, Jeremiah proclaimed that spiritual decline fueled the other areas of disintegration. Judah attempted to worship God and idols at the same time (2:1–4:4). They thought the mere existence of Temple observances guaranteed divine favor (7:1–8:3; 26:1–15). Some concluded that Jerusalem was destroyed because idols had not been venerated enough (44:15–19). Obviously, Judah was a nation in full retreat from its covenant obligations.

AUTHOR, DATE, AND AUDIENCE

Unlike many Old Testament books, Jeremiah includes specific information about its composition. The text claims that it contains Jeremiah's words (1:1), and indeed there are

3

several first-person ("I") passages (1:4–19; 2:1; etc.). At the same time, the book includes third-person passages in which the prophet is called "he" (7:1; 11:1; etc.). In 36:32 the text states that Baruch, a scribe and follower of Jeremiah, wrote some of Jeremiah's messages at his dictation. It is quite likely that Baruch wrote the third-person passages found in the book. He probably composed the final form of the prophecy after Jeremiah's death, or perhaps even collaborated with him before that time. If this proposed authorial option is correct, then it is likely that the book was completed by no later than 550 B.C., and probably several years sooner.

Jeremiah was finished at about the same time as 1 and 2 Kings, books that include material nearly identical to Jeremiah 52:1–34 (2 Kings 24:18–25:30).

Both Jeremiah and 1 and 2 Kings addressed a Jewish audience living between the loss of their nation in 587 B.C. and a return to their homeland in 538 B.C. This audience needed to know why the terrible defeat occurred. The older members needed to take responsibility for their sins, while the younger generation needed to avoid their elders' mistakes. Every segment of the audience also needed to understand that exile was not God's final word. Hope still existed, for the Lord promised to restore the nation some time in the future.

Don't just think about Jeremiah being written to people of long ago. Put yourself in their place. Formulate parallels between their situation and yours. Think about how the book's words apply to you. Ask yourself what God would have you do to obey His Word.

THE BOOK'S CONTENTS

Although Jeremiah jumps backward and forward in time, the book does have specific themes that shape it as a whole.

MAJOR THEMES IN JEREMIAH

Jeremiah 1:1–19 recounts the prophet's call to ministry, announces the book's time frame, main characters, major themes, and basic conflicts.

Jeremiah 2–29 expresses the Lord's displeasure with Judah's sin.

Jeremiah 30–33 offers promises of renewal and restoration and prophecy of a New Covenant (31:31–34).

Jeremiah 34–51 describes the demise and fall of Judah, promises judgment for sinful Gentile nations, provides an account of the fall of Jerusalem, and the fate of the Davidic dynasty.

In Leviticus 26 and Deuteronomy 27; 28, God, through Moses, warned of the punishment Jeremiah witnessed.

JEREMIAH'S THEOLOGY

As could be expected, Jeremiah's theology revolves around his view of God. In Jeremiah, God is the sovereign Lord who calls and equips the prophet with infallible words (1:1–19). God loves Israel, and calls them to Himself (2:1–4:4). God is righteous, so He insists on justice and kindness (7:1–15). The Lord is the one who judges sin, whether that sin occurs in Judah or some other country (chaps. 34–51). Yet God is also the one who forgives and promises a New Covenant (31:31–34). God is the one who will send the Savior (23:1–8).

Theology simply means "the study of God." A person's theology is what he or she believes about God. Christians seek to allow God's Word—Scripture—to shape their thinking about God. They want God's revelation of who He is, to be their guide to understanding and relating to Him.

Based on this exalted notion of God, Jeremiah formulates statements about human beings. Sadly, the human heart is sick and beyond care unless God intervenes (17:9–10). People break covenant with God (2:1–17). They worship idols (10:1–16). Therefore, over one hundred times, the prophet calls upon them "to repent," which literally means "to turn around" or "to change." Such change can only come when they seek the Lord.

There is no question in Jeremiah's mind that some day a righteous, penitent people of God will emerge. This group will follow the Savior (23:1–8). They will know God and will serve the Lord with all their hearts (31:31–34). This group will be what Judah should have been, for they will be faithful like Jeremiah. Thus, the future is bright for God's servants.

Despite this hopeful prospect, however, the book emphasizes God's judgment in the near future. This punishment is based on rebellion against God's kind and gracious covenant. Judah chooses disobedience and idolatry, which is the same thing as choosing judgment. God is patient, even slow to judge, but His righteousness demands a response to sin.

JEREMIAH IN THE REST OF THE BIBLE

Jeremiah has strategic importance for the rest of the Bible. Although his prophecies are cited in Daniel 9:2 and his lament for Josiah is noted in 2 Chronicles 35:25, perhaps its significance is most evident in the New Testament. Jesus states in Luke 22:20 that the Last Supper inaugurates the New Covenant in His blood. Likewise, Hebrews 8:1–13 cites Jeremiah 31:31–34 as part of a larger discussion of Jesus mediating the New Covenant through His death and resurrection. Clearly, the New Testament writers conclude that Jeremiah 31:31–34 looks forward to Christ's work on the cross and to the creation of a faithful people of God. In this way Jeremiah provides a strategic link between the Old and New Testaments.

"In the first year of his reign, I, Daniel, understood from the Scriptures, according to the word of the Lord given to Jeremiah the prophet, that the desolation of Jerusalem would last seventy years" (Dan. 9:2).

JEREMIAH AND TODAY'S WORLD

Jeremiah has much to say to both the secular world and to the church. To those outside the people of God, the book offers the Christ who can be their righteousness (23:1–8). It also informs the adherents of other religions that the Lord alone is God, and must be worshiped in the manner set forth in the inspired Scriptures (10:1–25).

God's people ought to note and avoid Judah's example. Faithfulness is a natural and reasonable response to the loving God. If this faithfulness does not characterize the church, then even the Lord's chosen ones may expect to experience God's chastening discipline. On the other hand, believers can count on God's forgiveness when real repentance marks a life. They can also expect that God will stand with them as He stood with Jeremiah in his many trials, temptations, disappointments, and persecutions. The Lord is always with the believer. God cannot fail to guide and encourage the called ones.

One must do more than be sincere in one's beliefs; one must turn to the living God of the Bible. Only judgment attends adherence to other gods.

THE GOD WHO CALLS (1:1–19)

GOD CALLS THE PROPHET (1:1–3)

This passage relates the Lord's summoning of Jeremiah to be a prophet. While doing so, God explained what Jeremiah had to preach and listed those who will oppose him. In this way the book's main points are introduced in its very first segment. What can we say about the God who calls?

Jeremiah was born in approximately 648 B.C. and grew up in the village of Anathoth, about two miles from Jerusalem.

The names of the kings mentioned here indicate that Jeremiah was a prophet about 627–587 B.C. These were tumultuous times spiritually, politically, and economically. Jeremiah's ministry spanned from Judah's last righteous king (Josiah; 640–609 B.C.) to Judah's last actual king (Zedekiah; 597–587 B.C.). Jeremiah lived long enough to see Jerusalem destroyed by Babylon in 587 B.C., an event he predicted as the result of Judah's sin. Most importantly, Jeremiah viewed all these events as under God's sovereign control. God, not kings, rules human history.

GOD IS PERSONAL (1:4–10)

Jeremiah was about twenty years old when God called him to be a prophet.

God spoke with Jeremiah directly, personally. The Lord commanded him to be a prophet, then calmed his fears about his youth and inexperience. God also pledged His presence, which meant divine protection would guard Jeremiah. The Lord's presence would remain personal and abiding as long as the prophet lived. The same God who planned for him to be a prophet *from the womb* would guide and protect him all his life.

GOD PROTECTS HIS WORD (1:11–16)

Having promised to give Jeremiah words to say (1:9), the Lord then pledged to "watch over" those words to guarantee that what the prophet said would be true. Jeremiah should have confidence in the divine word. God also revealed that the prophet's message would be one of judgment primarily, yet would also include hope ("build and plant"). Jeremiah must preach the Bible's three great prophetic themes: sin, punishment, and restoration.

GOD PROTECTS THE PROPHET (1:17–19)

God did not deceive Jeremiah about the difficulty of his task. In fact, God said Jeremiah's opponents would include every strata of Judah's society—prophets, priests, people, and royalty. What would save him? Only the Lord's protection that is safeguarded by God's presence. With God's presence, Jeremiah would be an impregnable fortress. He must not be afraid. Rather, he must trust in the Lord, his only friend.

QUESTIONS TO GUIDE YOUR STUDY

1. Who helped Jeremiah write his prophesy?
2. Which early leaders of Israel foretold the disasters that Jeremiah lived through?
3. Which later prophet read Jeremiah's prophecy and learned how long the Babylonian exile would last?
4. At what point did God decide to call Jeremiah as a prophet?

THE GOD WHO INSTRUCTS THE PROPHET (CHAPS. 2–6)

These chapters describe the Lord's first extended words to the prophet. In a series of instructional passages, Jeremiah heard God's concerns before actually preaching in chapter 7. What he learned was troubling. God's chosen people had forsaken the Lord for worthless idols. They must turn to God ("repent"), or judgment was inevitable.

ISRAEL IS A FAITHLESS SPOUSE (2:1–3:5)

God's comments are harsh, even shocking. Israel is compared to a faithless, straying, adulterous spouse. This infidelity is unwarranted, since the Lord has been faithful, constant, and truthful to Israel. Jeremiah learned that God's anger at the chosen people has foundations; it is understandable. How has Israel gotten into such a state?

"There I will give her back her vineyards, and will make the Valley of Achor a door of hope.
There she will sing as in the days of her youth,
as in the day she came up out of Egypt" (Hos. 2:15).

Israel Has Forgotten the Devotion of Her Youth (2:1–3)

In its youth, or in the Exodus account, Israel followed the Lord because it loved the Lord. God responded by providing for and protecting Israel. Clearly, *commitment solely to God* was, "the devotion of your youth." Now the commitment is gone.

Israel Has Grown Ungrateful to the Lord (2:4–8)

Despite all God's kindnesses, the people have turned to idols. Theological amnesia has overcome them. Priests, people, prophets, and kings alike have forgotten God's great acts in Israel's history. Forgetfulness left unattended has rotted into ingratitude.

Israel Has Changed Its God (2:9–13)

God charges Israel with desertion. This changing of allegiance from God to so-called gods that are in reality worthless is foolish. Such false deities cannot save. Israel has traded a constant source of help for a cracked, leaking source.

Israel Ignores Discipline (2:14–19)

Because of their sins, the Lord has allowed other countries to take property and territory from Israel. Despite their suffering, though, no changes occur. The people remained steadfast in their destructive attitudes and actions.

Israel Denies Wrongdoing (2:20–28)

At this stage of its history, nothing is more damaging to Israel than refusing to repent. Unfortunately, Israel claimed to be doing nothing wrong. They took this attitude even though they worshiped other gods routinely.

Israel Mistreats the Poor (2:29–37)

Not only has Israel been faithless to God; it has also been cruel to the poor and helpless in its midst. Forgetting the Lord, ignoring discipline, and denying its sins lead Israel to do evil. The whole society has become corrupt, for the people recognize no authority higher than themselves. Judgment can be expected, and it may fall at any time.

Israel Sleeps Around (3:1–5)

Israel tried to retain God's blessings while loving other gods. This impossible scenario defiled the land. God must punish this behavior. Benefits must be withheld. Israel whined when punished, yet has not come to its senses or accepted its responsibilities.

"But you trusted in your beauty and played the harlot because of your fame, and you poured out your harlotries on every passer-by who might be willing" (Ezek. 16:15, NASB).

Jeremiah represents God as a fountain of living waters. God's people have left Him for broken cisterns that can't hold water. (2:13). Compare this figure of speech with one that Jesus used to describe Himself: "But whoever drinks the water I give him will never thirst. Indeed, the water I give him will become in him a spring of water welling up to eternal life" (John 4:14).

Pride and ignorance make a deadly combination.

- *Israel has broken its covenant vows to the*
- *Lord. Its idolatry has led to pride, denial,*
- *cruelty, immorality, and bitterness. God*
- *will punish such sins so that wickedness will*
- *not prevail.*

ISRAEL HAS TIME TO CHANGE (3:6–4:4)

There is no question that Israel's situation looked bleak. Gladly mired in covenantal infidelity, it seemed headed toward an inevitable date with judgment. In this text the Lord informed Jeremiah that such is not the case. There is still time for Israel to repent, to change its ways and seek the Lord. Judgment is *not* inevitable.

The Past Places Judah in Peril (3:6–10)

Early in Jeremiah's ministry (c. 627–609 B.C.), the Lord informed the prophet that Israel and Judah have worshiped idols. This behavior continued for centuries. Therefore, God sent Assyria to conquer Israel, the ten northern tribes, in 722 B.C. Over a century has passed, but Judah has learned nothing from watching God's judgment on Israel. Its ongoing infidelity makes the nation vulnerable to invasion and destruction.

Idols were representations of gods. Those who used idols in worship accepted the reality of the gods depicted in the idols. The Bible states that there is only one God, and He commands that no images be made of Him (see Exod. 20:3, 4).

The Present Offers Judah a Fresh Start (3:11–14)

God invited the people to return to Him. God is gracious, merciful, and kind. If Judah will acknowledge, confess, and return to God, then the Lord will forgive. But a fresh start is dependent on a change of heart.

The Future Will be Bright for Judah (3:15–18)

Now God indicated that there would be a time when the people will change. They will be given good leaders, and they will return to Jerusalem. Evil hearts will be changed by the Lord. The question is whether *Jeremiah's generation* will enjoy these benefits. At this point the answer is "no."

God Calls the People to Repentance (3:19–25)

God freely offered choice blessings to the chosen people. It is not the Lord's wish to judge. When God called, however, the people chose to wallow in the filth and shame of idolatry. Grace was spurned. God's kindness was ignored.

Repentance Requires a New Heart (4:1–4)

No one can repent without a changed heart. Therefore, God's demands for change are linked to the people "circumcising their hearts." Biblical faith, in both the Old and New Testaments, begins internally, then flows outward in an obedient life. Godliness requires a complete commitment. Since the people refuse to make such a commitment, wrath awaits the unfaithful, unbending nation.

- *God gives sinners time to repent. Before*
- *judgment comes, the Lord warns, calls, and*
- *teaches. Punishment need not occur and will*
- *not befall those who turn their hearts and*
- *lives toward the Creator.*

GOD IS BRINGING DESTRUCTION (4:5–31)

Israel has time to repent, but it does not have forever to do so. God will send an as-yet-

God still calls people to repentance. In Christ He bids all people to turn from their sins and open their hearts to Christ. Repentance is a daily practice that keeps one's relationship with God strong and vital (1 John 1:9, 10).

Ethical implications of circumcision can be observed in the metaphorical usage of the term. The uncircumcised are those who are insensitive to God's leadership. Circumcision of the heart implies total devotion to God: "Circumcise the foreskin of your heart, and be stiff-necked no longer" (Deut. 10:16, NKJV).

unspecified army to defeat and destroy them. This news should spur the nation toward change. Instead, it only moves the prophet to have concern for his hearers. No repentance results.

The Judgment Will Lead to Lamenting (4:5–13)

The army that will invade the land will be like a fierce lion devouring his prey. Kings, princes, priests, and prophets will be appalled at what will unfold. There will be no peace for the adulterous people, only sorrow and lamenting.

The Threat Should Lead to Change (4:14–18)

Jerusalem—indeed, all of Judah—needs to wash its hearts of sin (see 4:3–4). It is time for the nation to admit that its social, economic, and military difficulties are a direct result of rebellion against the Lord. It is time to see the situation as an opportunity to come back to the One who loves the nation the most.

Refusal to Change Is Foolish (4:19–31)

Israel's' unwillingness to repent proves that the people are foolish, devoid of knowledge. By now they should know the Lord, but all they know is the Lord's displeasure. The coming devastation will be like a reversal of creation. Israel's cities, even Jerusalem, will be as desolate as the earth while it was formless and void. Although Israel seeks help from other gods, no help will come. Severe pain like that of childbirth will overwhelm the people.

Verse 23 describes coming conditions like those described in Genesis 1:2 where the earth was formless and void. Jeremiah looked to the heavens and saw not light but darkness—a reversal of creation.

- *God will not destroy Judah all at once.*
- *Smaller punishments will come first to*
- *encourage the nation to return to God. Refus-*
- *ing to heed early warnings will lead to the*
- *Lord taking sterner measures.*

GOD WILL REMOVE THE WICKED (5:1–31)

Before Jeremiah can accept Judah's destruction, he must know whether all the people have become corrupt. Certainly, God will spare the nation if enough righteous persons exist. Surely the Lord will not destroy the good with the evil! Sadly, Jeremiah learned that intercession is fruitless, since the whole country has grown corrupt.

There Are No Righteous Persons in Judah (5:1–9)

As was the case with Sodom, there are too few righteous persons in Judah to withhold judgment. The land is filled with dishonesty, religious hypocrisy, and injustice. Every level of society participates in these sins. Therefore, God can see no reason to pardon Judah.

The People Have Lied about God (5:10–13)

The people are so steeped in sin that they mistake God's mercy for weakness. They have grown overconfident and complacent in their transgressions, and now they believe the Lord will do nothing to stop them. They say that God is anemic and uncaring about evil. In other words, they think God is like them.

This passage is reminiscent of what God told Abraham regarding Sodom and Gommorah (Gen. 18:16–33).

"When God saw their deeds, that they turned from their wicked way, then God relented concerning the calamity which He had declared He would bring upon them. And He did not do it" (Jon. 3:10, NASB).

The Prophetic Word Will Consume the Wicked (5:14–29)

Since the chosen people comfort themselves with lies, the Lord will make Jeremiah's words a consuming fire and the people to whom he speaks will be as wood. These words predict a terrible invasion by a mighty army. They will promise exile and other means of divine punishment. They will condemn the polluted hearts of the defiant nation. They will preach God's covenant and God's revealed word, which will expose the nations' waywardness and hatred of the truth. By the time Jeremiah's ministry ends, Jerusalem will be in ruins and the populace will be scattered. God will be avenged for Judah's unfaithfulness.

The People Love Lying Priests and Prophets (5:30–31)

Few things are as dangerous to the nations as untrustworthy spiritual leaders. Priests who do not teach the word cut off the people from their only infallible guide for wise living. Prophets who preach whatever they think their audiences want to hear obliterate a country's moral conscience. Tragically, Judah loved such religious officials. They committed spiritual suicide by clinging to teachers who instructed them to ignore the truth.

When spiritual leaders don't tell their people God's truth, it's like a physician giving a clean bill of health to someone with a serious disease. Only the consequences are far more severe.

■ *There was no reason to believe that God*
■ *would spare Jeremiah's audience. No signs of*
■ *spiritual life were evident. When a country*
■ *becomes this corrupt, then judgment can be*
■ *expected.*

JEREMIAH MUST TEST THE PEOPLE
(6:1–30)

Before Jeremiah works among the people, one more lesson remains. The Lord's message will fill him, and the message will test Judah's motives and actions. The prophet seems excited about sharing God's word. He seems nearly ready to address the people.

The Nation Should Prepare for Invasion (6:1–8)

Because Judah fails to repent, they should prepare for a foreign army to terrorize them. The people have embraced violence, destruction, sickness, and spiritual wounds rather than righteousness. Jerusalem has become known more for wickedness than for being the focal point of covenantal faith.

In verse 8, Jeremiah likens Jerusalem to a well of fresh water that's always flowing. Except what continually flows from Jerusalem is wickedness.

The Nation Rejects God's Word (6:9–15)

Why did Judah refuse to change? Chiefly because they did not value God's word. Instead, they were greedy for gain, eager for soothing sermons, and unashamed of their activities. They preferred to ignore divinely empowered prophets. Jeremiah must learn to endure rejection of his messages.

Jeremiah used the picture of a physician (6:14) who has healed the brokenness of God's people in a superficial way—saying "peace, peace" when there is no peace.

The Nation Refuses to Walk in God's Ways (6:16–26)

God's people had no intention of following the example of faithful persons in the past. They would not walk in the established paths of righteousness, which is the logical consequence of refusing to believe God's word. Therefore, God will send a destroying army against them. Terror will be the result of rebellion against divine revelation.

Jeremiah declared that the mourning Jerusalem would experience when God's judgment comes is like that when one loses an only son (6:26).

17

Jeremiah's Ministry Will Test the Nation (6:27–30)

Whether they know it or not, how they react to Jeremiah's ministry will be Judah's ultimate test. God will not judge them based on their military, economic, or political prowess. God will not assess them based on external considerations. Rather, the Lord will determine their future by how well they respond to Jeremiah's messages. Their greatest test is whether they believe the messenger whom God has sent.

- *The mark of a great people is their commit-*
- *ment to God and God's word. Israel failed in*
- *this most important of all tests. By failing to*
- *repent, they chose defeat and judgment.*

QUESTIONS TO GUIDE YOUR STUDY

1. What had the people of Judah done to separate themselves from God?
2. What happened to Israel—the ten northern tribes?
3. How had Judah's "physicians" engaged in malpractice?
4. Jeremiah likened Jerusalem to a well. What kind of water issues from this well?

Jeremiah's Early Work (Chaps. 7–10)

Now the book moves to Jeremiah's practice of the principles God taught him in chapters 1–6. Of course, the earlier chapters may also have been presented to an audience, but the book presents them as a guide for the prophet. Jeremiah became more personally involved with the people. He preached, counseled, challenged, and generally labored to turn his nation back to God. By so doing he fulfilled the divine calling he received in chapter 1. Six episodes mark the beginning stages of Jeremiah's work.

THE FIRST TEMPLE SERMON (7:1–8:3)

Jeremiah did not have to wait long before he began to test the people (cp. 6:27–30). God sent him out to preach at the Temple, the holiest site in Judah. What he said would not be popular. Thus, the opposition promised in 1:17–19 did occur. Preaching the truth did not lead to acclaim or appreciation for him. His sermon unfolded in six parts.

The People Put Their Faith in the Temple (7:1–7)

God positioned Jeremiah at the Temple gate so the prophet could confront those who came to services there. What they heard must have startled them. Jeremiah commanded them to amend their ways. They believed that their great building ensured their relationship with the Lord. They thought that a fine worship center, high attendance, and good offerings are all that God requires. Sadly, they placed their faith in a building, not in God.

"'Get yourself ready! Stand up and say to them whatever I command you. Do not be terrified by them, or I will terrify you before them. Today I have made you a fortified city, an iron pillar and a bronze wall to stand against the whole land—against the kings of Judah, its officials, its priests and the people of the land. They will fight against you but will not overcome you, for I am with you and will rescue you,' declares the Lord" (Jer. 1:17–19).

Three temples are mentioned in Scripture. The first was built by Solomon in 966 B.C. and destroyed in 587 B.C. This is the Temple mentioned in Jeremiah. A second Temple was built 520–516 B.C. by exiles who had returned from Babylon. The third Temple was a vast expansion of the second Temple. It was finished in A.D. 66 only to be destroyed by the Romans in A.D. 70. The third Temple is the one that was standing during Jesus' lifetime.

The people saw the Temple as a sanctuary. They believed that God would not allow His Temple to be destroyed. But God reminded the people that He abandoned Shiloh, the place where the tabernacle stood (7:12).

"He abandoned the tabernacle of Shiloh, the tent he had set up among men" (Ps. 78:60).

"If anyone sees his brother commit a sin that does not lead to death, he should pray and God will give him life. I refer to those whose sin does not lead to death. There is a sin that leads to death. I am not saying that he should pray about that" (1 John 5:16).

The People Corrupt the Temple Through Corrupt Worship (7:8–11)

The very Temple the so-called worshipers trusted in was turned into a den of robbers whenever services were held. How so? Because they broke the Ten Commandments, refused to repent, then acted as if their "worship" pleased God. Worse still, they offered sacrifices to Baal, the fertility god. They believed they could worship the Lord as one God among many despite what Moses taught.

Their Behavior Will Lead to the Temple's Destruction (7:12–15)

God is not bound to a specific place. Israel's sin led to the destruction of Shiloh, an earlier worship center (cp. 1 Sam. 4:10). When Judah is defeated, the Temple will be destroyed. Those who pretend to worship while ignoring God's word can expect to suffer Shiloh's fate.

God Will Not Heed Intercession on Their Behalf (7:16–20)

Judah's sins were so terrible that God told the prophet not to intercede for them. Prayer would not halt the approaching devastation. God's mind was set. Wrath will come upon all who worship idols.

External Observances Do Not Impress God (7:21–26)

Mere external religious rites, however consistent and elaborate, do not impress God. Sacrifice is not the sum total of Israel's faith. From the very start the Lord's chief expectation was obedience from the heart. The people had forgotten the heart of God's law, had made useless sacrifices, and had felt spiritual doing so. God had told them these truths, but the Lord's messengers had been ignored.

Judgment Will Make an End of Judah
(7:27–8:3)

God knew that the people would not pay attention to Jeremiah's sermons. Still, he must preach so that God's righteousness will be evident. In the end, the people will be destroyed because of wickedness that includes child sacrifices. Those who kill the innocent will lose their own lives when every city in Judah lies in ruins.

- *God's love for the people deserved a response*
- *of faith and obedience. External religion*
- *alone does not please a holy, personal God.*

A SERMON ON THE REJECTED LAW
(8:4–17)

Jeremiah's second message deals with the people's rejection of the divinely revealed Mosaic Law. Their attitude about God's written Word was similar to how they thought about the Temple. That is, they believed that the possession of the Scriptures guaranteed the Lord's pleasure. Therefore, God sent Jeremiah to expose their mistaken notion.

The People Are Ignorant of God's Word
(8:4–7)

God said that the people had willfully, repeatedly, and gladly continued in their sins. They feigned surprise at this news, which demonstrated their ignorance of what the Scriptures teach. Those who do not obey God's Word have no idea what it means.

Religious Leaders Misinterpret the Scriptures
(8:8–12)

Part of the people's problem in obeying the Law was that their teachers did not teach it faithfully

"Evil men do not understand justice, but those who seek the Lord understand it fully" (Prov. 28:5).

Every Christian must strive to interpret the Bible accurately. To do so, one must understand a passage's immediate and broader context. It is important to read a text in light of the verses surrounding it, as well as in light of the whole of Scripture. Avoid grabbing a single isolated phrase and interpreting that phrase without knowing the context of which it is a part.

or properly. They turned the truth into lies, and told the nation it was fine to continue their wicked deeds. Since they felt no shame over leading others astray, the Lord would punish them.

Believing Lies Leads to Destruction (8:13–17)
There was no hope for Judah if they continued to insist on listening to falsehood instead of heeding God's warnings. They might long for peace; yet they would experience destruction. Lies do not lead to freedom, for only truth removes the bondage of sin.

- *Those who believe God's Word obey it.*
- *Rejecting divine revelation and teaching*
- *others to do so will inevitably lead to divine*
- *judgment.*

JEREMIAH'S LIFE AMID A DECEITFUL PEOPLE (8:18–9:9)

So far the prophet had not suffered persecution for his messages. This situation could not hold, however, since the nation was deceitful and treacherous. Jeremiah must be on his guard. Those who reject God will also reject God's messenger.

"Brethren, my heart's desire and my prayer to God for them is for their salvation" (Rom. 10:1, NASB). Like Jeremiah, Paul longed for his people, Israel, to come to faith in the Lord.

Jeremiah Mourns for His People (8:18–22)
There can be no question that Jeremiah loved his people and wished they would be saved. Their wickedness prevented their being forgiven. They could not be healed, because they did not return to God, the one who could make them whole. This reality broke Jeremiah's heart as he prayed for the nation. He asked, "Is there no balm in Gilead? . . . no physician there?" (8:22) The answer to Jeremiah's rhetorical ques-

tion is, "Yes, there is balm in Gilead." He is God, but He will not force healing on those who will not be healed.

The People Are Deceitful (9:1–6)

God informed Jeremiah that he must be on guard against these deceitful people. This text is the first indication that he would be in danger later. The prophet must learn to trust in God alone. He had no other hope; no other security; no other protection.

Gilead was famous especially for its flocks and herds, and for the balm of Gilead, an aromatic and medicinal preparation, probably derived from the resin of a small balsam tree.

The God of Truth Must Judge a Lying People (9:7–9)

The people's lies caused social injustice, so the just and fully honest Lord must act. God mourned for the nation no less than Jeremiah did. Still, constant sin cannot be treated lightly. The innocent cry out for help.

God used the picture of refining metal as He spoke of Judah (9:7). Metal is tested or assayed in order to separate what is pure from the dross that has been mixed with the metal.

■ *Although Jeremiah had to preach condemna-*
■ *tion he still loved the people. Although God*
■ *loved Israel, they must still be judged. Nei-*
■ *ther God nor His prophet rejoiced in the*
■ *coming devastation.*

JEREMIAH'S GRIEF OVER JUDAH (9:10–26)

What was to happen in the future now began to affect Jeremiah more and more. He realized that the punishment would be terrible. At the same time, he continued to know that repentance would stave off judgment, a fact that made Judah's hardness of heart all the more difficult to bear.

Judah's Judgment Will be Thorough, Yet Just (9:10–22)

Eventually, Jerusalem will be reduced to a heap of rubble, a desolate wasteland. Forsaking the Law and serving other gods can only lead to grief. Shame will lead to tears, wailing, and regret, though only the prophet sees that now.

Knowing God Matters Most (9:23–24)

Judah suffered from emphasizing the wrong things. Rather than boasting of money and power, they ought to revel in knowing the Lord. If they knew God, they would realize that God exercises love, kindness, and justice. If they knew God, they would imitate Him. Nothing matters more than knowing God and doing God's will.

Knowing God requires understanding God's character, aims, and will. God is loving, kind, gracious, powerful, righteous, patient, and holy. Those who trust Him discover that the Scriptures tell the truth about Him.

All Nations Will be Judged (9:25–26)

None of the countries around Judah were more righteous than they. Therefore, the Creator of all peoples would assess all peoples. Their hearts are as corrupt as the covenant nation's heart, so they will endure the same judgment.

■ *Knowing and serving God would remove the*
■ *certainty of judgment from Judah and the*
■ *other nations. A merciful God takes no*
■ *pleasure in condemning the wicked.*

IDOLATRY AND EXILE (10:1–25)

With each message he delivered, the prophet became more aware of the connection between idolatry and judgment and between sin and exile. In this segment, Jeremiah confessed God's incomparability. He also emphasized the uselessness of images of gods, and underscored the losses Judah incurred by worshiping worthless things. Jeremiah realized that when the covenant people bow to other nations' gods, the Lord turns them over to those countries.

Judah Must Reject All Other Gods (10:1–5)

This passage indicates that Judah must not mimic the worship patterns of their neighbors. These nations worshiped the works of their hands—mere images that cannot speak or walk. Therefore, the point is not that the Lord must be the only deity *for Judah* but that no other god truly exists.

There Is No God Like the Lord (10:6–10)

All nations should serve the Lord, for He alone is great, powerful, worthy of reverence, wise, living, and everlasting. Wise persons from all lands will recognize the Lord's incomparability. If they do not, then God's justifiable wrath will overcome them just as it will overwhelm Judah.

The Lord Is the Creator (10:11–16)

The Lord must be recognized as the only God. He alone made the world in power, through wisdom and by understanding. In contrast, people who serve idols are weak, foolish, and undiscerning. Their choice is between serving the One who created them or gods which they created themselves.

Idolatrous Judah Is Headed for Exile (10:17–25)

God will throw sinful Judah out of the land for their idolatry. Exile will cause great pain. Much of the blame for Judah's demise lay with their leaders, who had led the people away from God. Jeremiah himself searched his own heart and asked the Lord to correct him but to do so gently. He did not want to perish with Judah and the other nations that rejected the Lord.

The reference to "signs in the heavens" (v. 2) could refer to Babylonian religion which saw phenomena in the heavens as having implications for life on earth. Phenomena such as comets and eclipses were terrifying to those who looked to the heavens for guidance.

"See now that I myself am He! There is no god besides me" (Deut. 32:39).

■ *The Lord is not merely the national deity of*
■ *Israel. Rather, He is the Creator, the Lord of*
■ *creation, the only living God, the one who*
■ *deserves to be worshiped by all persons. All*
■ *nations are accountable to Him and are loved*
■ *by Him.*

QUESTIONS TO GUIDE YOUR STUDY

1. When God called Jeremiah to be a prophet, what did He promise?
2. What were the people's attitudes toward and belief about their Temple?
3. How many different temples existed in the history of Israel?
4. Jeremiah prophesied that God would abandon the Temple. What earlier action did Jeremiah cite to show that this would not be the first time God had abandoned a place of worship which He established?

JEREMIAH'S CONFRONTATIONS WITH GOD (CHAPS. 11–20)

In this section the prophet's ministry continued, yet not without external pressures and internal struggles. Spiritual depression gripped Jeremiah as he encountered severe persecution. He wondered why the wicked prosper, and challenged the way God treated him. Five crises result from these confrontations, each one of which aided Jeremiah's growing commitment to the Lord and the ministry to which he was called.

JEREMIAH'S NAIVETE (CHAPS. 11–12)

Despite earlier warnings to expect opposition (1:17–19; 9:1–3), Jeremiah did not readily accept adversity. He seemed to assume that he could win over the people to his point of view. When he learned otherwise, he questioned why the wicked prospered. This naive approach to his ministry must give way to a more mature walk with God and a more realistic view of the nation's sinfulness.

Israel's History of Covenant Breaking (11:1–17)

God asked Jeremiah to deliver a message devoted to a critique of Israel's history. God had blessed the people at every stage of their existence, yet He had this kindness spurned by the chosen nation. Because of their disobedience to the covenant principles, Israel must face the consequences of their actions. They must leave the land God had given them. None of the gods in whom they trusted could deliver them from the living God who had commanded their destruction.

Jeremiah pictured himself as a gentle lamb being led to the slaughter—as one cut off from the land of the living. This picture appears in Isaiah's prophecy (53:7–8) and is a description of the Suffering Servant—Jesus, the Messiah.

Jeremiah's Enemies Plot Against Him (11:18–23)

To his great dismay, Jeremiah's life was threatened by men from his hometown. If God had not revealed their plot and protected him, the prophet would have died. As Jeremiah trusted in the Lord's ability to judge the wicked, he learned that God would indeed punish these enemies. The Lord, therefore, kept His promise to deliver Jeremiah from his foes (1:17–19). God's presence shielded him from those who hated the divine message and the chosen messenger.

Jeremiah's Complaint about the Wicked (12:1–4)

Based upon his belief in God's righteousness, Jeremiah asked how God could allow wicked persons to prosper. Such people rejected the Lord, yet the Lord planted them in the land. These sinners were defiling the land, and Jeremiah wanted them punished. He wanted no further opposition.

God's Challenge to Jeremiah (12:5–13)

God challenged Jeremiah to prepare for worse times as well as to consider how the Lord felt about the situation. Jeremiah had much harder experiences on the way. While he got ready for this eventuality, he must realize that God was tearing down everything He had built. God must forsake beloved Israel to the enemy. Clearly, judging the nation did not thrill the Lord, so Jeremiah must not clamor for his opponent's demise. Horrible devastation will come soon enough.

God's Promise for the Future (12:14–17)

Throughout the book of Jeremiah the point is made that God punishes in order to restore and renew. The Lord is compassionate, always ready to heal all nations, not just Israel. A new exodus will occur in which scattered Israel will be gathered back to the land.

- God's sovereignty and compassion are an
- integrated whole. As the prophet grasped a
- greater sense of God's nature, he gained a
- more mature vision for his own ministry.
- Punishment has a higher purpose than the
- removal of personal enemies.

A PERCEIVED BETRAYAL BY GOD (CHAPS. 13–15)

No sooner did one crisis pass than another one arose. Personal crisis takes many forms, and no one crisis affects everyone the same. Yet betrayal at the hands of a trusted friend is almost always devastating. Few can easily forget these painful experiences. In these chapters, Jeremiah raised questions about whether God can be trusted. As he probed God's character, however, he learned that the Lord may be trusted and that he himself must repent of unbelief.

Israel Is a Ruined Nation (13:1–11)

This passage begins the book's description of symbolic acts which the prophet performs to proclaim God's word. Jeremiah bought a belt, buried it, and noted how it was ruined. Thus, he learned that Judah is a ruined nation due to idolatry. God's people have earned the punishment that must surely come upon them.

Israel Is a Drunken Nation (13:12–14)

Through the use of a proverb, the prophet declared how utterly out of control the people have become. They will be as helpless against

The belt has been variously described as a loincloth or a girdle. It symbolized the closeness between God and Judah which once existed and in which Judah took pride. Taking the belt off and burying it showed that the close relationship between God and Judah no longer existed.

their foes as a drunken person. In fact, God will make them clueless about their future. Since they do not heed the Lord's warnings, they will be given over to their own stupidity.

Jeremiah's Exhortation to the Nation (13:15–27)

Even after all God has said about Judah's inevitable collapse, the prophet still sought to turn the people's hearts. He tried to break down their arrogance. He encouraged them to glorify God before it was too late. He wept over their stubbornness, the fate of their monarchs, the ingrained nature of their sin, and God's need to punish their shameless acts. No one could accuse Jeremiah of a lack of concern for his hearers. The question is whether the people shared his burden.

Judah's Drought and Jeremiah's Intercession (14:1–22)

Punishment began with a terrible drought that left the land reeling. Moved with pity, the prophet asked God to relent. God refused to do so, and even told Jeremiah not to pray for these wicked ones (cp. 7:16; 11:14). God had already decided to chastise the rebellious nation and their lying prophets and priests. This decision moved Jeremiah to pray despite what God had decreed. He seemed unable to accept that the decision to punish was final.

God's Refusal to Answer Jeremiah's Prayers (15:1–9)

God informed Jeremiah that not even Moses or Samuel could pray Judah out of their dilemma. The judgment is just, and the matter is closed. The fault lay in the people, not in the Lord or the prophet. What discouraged Jeremiah was that he must continue to preach, knowing that he

"But Moses sought the favor of the LORD his God. 'O LORD,' he said, 'why should your anger burn against your people, whom you brought out of Egypt with great power and a mighty hand? . . . Turn from your fierce anger; relent and do not bring disaster on your people. Remember your servants Abraham, Isaac and Israel, to whom you swore by your own self: I will make your descendants as numerous as the stars in the sky and I will give your descendants all this land I promised them, and it will be their inheritance forever.' Then the LORD relented and did not bring on his people the disaster he had threatened" (Exod. 32:11–14).

"Then Samuel took a suckling lamb and offered it up as a whole burnt offering to the LORD. He cried out to the LORD on Israel's behalf, and the LORD answered him" (1 Sam. 7:9).

would not be successful in turning their hearts by changing their minds.

Jeremiah's Complaint Against God (15:10–18)

God's answer hardly satisfied the prophet. Rather than accept the Lord's response to his earnest intercession, Jeremiah chose to lament his own role in life. Although he had tried to help the people, they despised him. Worse still, he believed God promised him good but only bad had come. He claimed to have suffered much, while the Lord had done little. Therefore, he implied strongly that God was "like a deceptive brook" (15:18), or one that is an unreliable source of sustenance. In other words, the prophet blamed God for his pain. He had become too much like the sinful people to whom he ministered.

Biblical characters often offer laments. A lament is a complaint offered in faith that the Lord will act on behalf of the one praying. Laments show faith in that they focus on God as the One who can change the circumstances. At times, though, laments can degenerate into sheer complaint, as is the case here.

God's Call to Repentance (15:19–21)

The Lord did not consider Jeremiah's complaint valid. Indeed, he told the prophet to repent. Jeremiah must separate the precious from the worthless. He must choose between God's precious calling and worthless, self-serving opinions. Further, he must identify more with God than with the people if he wanted to be God's spokesman. As he did so, he could count on the Lord's protection, just as 1:17–19 already promised. If he wanted to serve, his only option was to trust solely in the One who called him in the first place.

God promised Jeremiah that if he would remain faithful, God would make Jeremiah like a bronze wall. The people might fight against him, but they would not prevail.

■ *God never abandons the faithful. Although*
■ *circumstances are difficult, even seemingly*
■ *unbearable, the Lord remains in loving con-*
■ *trol of the universe and every individual in it.*
■ *When believers doubt God's goodness, balk*
■ *at doing God's will, and blame God for life*
■ *being as God said it would be, then repen-*
■ *tance is necessary. Even believers sin and*
■ *need divine forgiveness.*

JEREMIAH'S PERSONAL RENEWAL (16:1–17:18)

Reconciliation rarely comes easily. Even when two estranged parties desire a better relationship, the healing may take time and effort. Although harsh words are exchanged in 15:15–21, God gave the prophet more work to do—almost as if nothing had happened. Jeremiah must find a way to obey God fully while ministering to a nation that will not encourage his faithfulness.

The Terrible Times Awaiting the People (16:1–18)

God often asked prophets to do symbolic acts to show God's concerns to the people. The most heart-rending example of symbolic prophecy is Hosea's marriage to Gomer, a prostitute (Hos. 1–3), a union that symbolized Israel's relationship to the Lord. Every symbolic act was calculated to make the audience ask why the messenger acted as he did.

Once again the prophet was told to act out God's message to Judah. This time he must carry out three strange commands. Each one separated Jeremiah further from the people. First, God ordered the prophet not to marry (16:1–4). Why? Because wives and children would be killed by invading armies used by the Lord to punish Israel's sins. Second, God told Jeremiah not to mourn the dead, since they are better off than the living given the coming devastation (16:5–7). Third, feasts are also off limits for the prophet (16:8, 9). Such celebrations amount to wishful thinking perpetuated by a decaying society. Jeremiah's behavior would give him a chance to confront the people with their need to repent (16:10–13). God assured Jeremiah that there remained hope for the people (16:14, 15), yet this brighter future would only arise out of the ashes of a destroyed Israel (16:16–18).

The Depths of Human Sin (16:19–17:11)

Part of Jeremiah's struggle in his relationship to God stemmed from his apparent belief that there must be some desire to repent on Israel's part. Thus, he did not want to stop praying for the people, to keep preaching harsh messages, or to withdraw from the normal activities.

Here God asserted that Israel's idolatry was carved upon their hearts (16:19–17:4). Therefore, Jeremiah must not trust in them at all (17:5–8). Trusting in God alone could make Jeremiah flourish. Indeed, the human heart is desperately wicked; it is incurably sick to the point that only God can understand its depths (17:9–11).

"For all have sinned and fall short of the glory of God" (Rom. 3:23).

Jeremiah's Prayer for Renewal (17:12–18)

Given God's explanation of human sinfulness, Jeremiah prayed for healing and deliverance. Further, he committed himself to more preaching based on God's promise to be with him. Finally, he asked the Lord to help him have courage. Of course, God had been sustaining him since chapter 1. God was certainly willing to remain faithful now.

■ *The crucial relationship between Lord and*
■ *servant has been restored. God has not*
■ *wavered in His commitment to Jeremiah, and*
■ *Jeremiah has (for now) accepted God's will*
■ *for his life.*

THE BURDEN OF CONSTANT OPPOSITION (17:19–18:23)

Human beings do not possess divine strength and perseverance. Therefore, continuous opposition and ongoing stress often cause even stout hearts to fail. As Jeremiah remained faithful to his calling, the nation remained equally faithful to their opposition. Eventually, this constant discord wore him down, which in turn led the prophet to express his pain to God.

The Necessity of Keeping the Sabbath Holy (17:19–27)

By Jeremiah's time, Israel had lived with God's command to rest on the Sabbath for more than eight hundred years (cp. Exod. 20:8–11). In fact, God's resting on the seventh day of Creation set an example that makes the Sabbath an integral part of human existence (cp. Gen. 2:1–3). Despite their familiarity with this standard, Jeremiah's compatriots failed to obey it. Instead, they worked as if God had said nothing about rest. God warned that such blatant materialism must stop, or an invading army would stop *all* of Jerusalem's activities. This message did nothing to endear Jeremiah to the people. His ministry remained difficult and unpopular.

Israel Is Like a Spoiled Pot (18:1–17)

As in 13:1–7 and 16:1–9, the Lord used a symbol to send a message to Israel. This time

God directed Jeremiah to go see a potter making a vessel. The potter shaped and reshaped the pot as he saw fit. In a similar manner, the Lord shaped Israel's future as He deemed appropriate. When Israel was obedient, then the Lord blessed them. When the nation worshiped other gods, God punished them. If the people repented of their sins, then God forgave and restored. Blessing was not automatic, yet their situation was never hopeless as long as repentance remained a possibility. Sadly, the people did not repent. Thus, the nation was spoiled and must be reshaped, this time for devastating judgment.

God is sovereign over all creation. The Lord is in loving control of each life. God shapes and reshapes each individual in a way that brings glory to His name. A wise person yields himself or herself to God's shaping.

Israel's Opposition to Jeremiah (18:18–23)

Such messages led to determined opposition. The people ignored the prophet's words and slandered him because they preferred to believe their religious leaders, all of whom thought the people were fine. Jeremiah prayed against these foes, asking the Lord to punish their treachery. The prophet had grown tired of the very people he asked the Lord to spare. He had told them the truth, for which they had discredited and abused him.

■ *Gradually the prophet lost patience with the*
■ *nation. No matter what he said or did, they*
■ *did not respond. Consistent ministry had,*
■ *sadly, drawn constant opposition that caused*
■ *constant pain.*

FIGHTING HIS CALLING (19:1–20:18)

It would seem that after enduring slander and avoiding plots against his life, surely Jeremiah could expect some peace and safety now. But no relief came. Jeremiah must preach and suffer again. His message remained harsh, so his opponents stayed active. Therefore, Jeremiah wondered why he should continue. He questioned whether God treated him fairly and wondered if the prophetic calling was worth pressing.

Israel Will Be Shattered (19:1–15)

Like 18:1–12, this chapter recounts a symbolic story involving pottery. In the first story the people still had time to repent, which meant that God could reshape them for blessing. Here, on the other hand, Jeremiah presented Judah as a jar that would, in fact, be shattered. A foreign army would lay siege to Jerusalem and destroy it. The nation's unwillingness to hear the prophetic word has guaranteed this disaster. Individuals may still repent, but the nation as a whole had run out of time.

Jeremiah Endures Suffering (20:1–6)

When Pashhur, "the chief officer in the temple of the LORD" (20:1), heard this sermon, he became enraged. He had Jeremiah beaten and placed in stocks. In response, the prophet declared that his antagonist would go into captivity in Babylon and die. Indeed, all who had believed lies would suffer at the hands of the Babylonians. Although he consistently told the truth, Jeremiah remained in peril all the time. He knew that his obedience led to suffering, and this knowledge gnawed at his sense of fairness.

Jeremiah Laments His Calling (20:7–18)

With great passion and extreme irony, Jeremiah stated what it meant to be an Old Testament prophet. Few texts in Scripture offer as vivid and realistic an account of this hazardous calling. Jeremiah felt deceived by God, insulted by the community, and ready to die. He knew that God puts His enemies to shame, but such vindication was less than comforting, since it only isolated him further from others. Given these circumstances, he had tried to stop preaching, only to discover that God's word was like a fire in his bones. Relief came only through preaching.

Thus, he preached on, yet felt the agony of doing so. Being faithful was the right thing to do; it was not, however, the easy thing to do. His willingness to forge ahead is a testimony to Jeremiah's faith.

■ *Not even unrelenting pressure and personal*
■ *doubts could stop Jeremiah's ministry. God*
■ *did not allow him to quit. Now the prophet*
■ *fully realized that his only hope was in the*
■ *Lord. He could not expect human support.*

QUESTIONS TO GUIDE YOUR STUDY

1. In what way was Jeremiah naive about his contemporaries?
2. What did Jeremiah's burying his belt symbolize?
3. What did Jeremiah do when God failed to respond to his intercessions?
4. What other Old Testament character was Jeremiah like in his candid conversations with God?

Even though at times Jeremiah felt an acute loneliness, he nevertheless experienced God standing by his side as a great champion.

Strong parallels exist between Jeremiah's response to his suffering and Job's response to the calamities Satan brought on him (Job 3:3–6).

"Today I have made you a fortified city, an iron pillar and a bronze wall to stand against the whole land—against the kings of Judah, its officials, its priests and the people of the land" (Jer. 1:18).

JEREMIAH'S CONFRONTATIONS WITH HIS ENEMIES (CHAPS. 21–29)

With his relationship with God solidified, Jeremiah now focused on confronting his opponents. God warned Jeremiah in 1:17–19 that kings, priests, princes, and people would be against him here. In this section, each of these groups heard God's word for them, and each one retaliated against the prophet. Each time, Jeremiah sought the Lord rather than blaming God for his situation. He had matured as a prophet and as a believer.

JEREMIAH OPPOSES THE KINGS (21:1–23:8)

During his forty-year ministry, Jeremiah served under five kings. Only Josiah, the first one, served and pleased the Lord. The other four differed in their personalities, but all were alike in their unwillingness to obey God. Given this sad history, Jeremiah looked forward to a perfect King who would save the people.

Here the account deals with Zedekiah, the last king of Judah (597–587 B.C.), an individual who had a very hard time following advice he knew to be accurate.

The Kingdom Will Perish (21:1–14)

The book of Jeremiah often jumps from one time frame to another, all the while expecting the reader to keep up with the changes. Of course, the original readers had no problem doing so, but today's readers need to be careful not to lose track of a passage's historical context.

As Babylon's armies invaded the land, Zedekiah asked the prophet if the Lord was planning to deliver the chosen nation. Clearly, the king had not been paying attention to Jeremiah's sermons! Of course, the prophet could offer no hope to the rebellious people and their wicked monarch. He could only advise them to surrender to the oncoming enemy. God's judgment will most certainly fall on the people because of their idolatry and upon the royal household because it has not administered justice. Zedekiah was engaging in wishful thinking.

David's House Will Be Left Desolate (22:1–12)

God sent Jeremiah to the king's house to remind the ruler of his obligations to the people and to the Lord. Kings are supposed to ensure justice, deliver the oppressed, and stand on the side of the weak and hurting. Because Judah's kings had not acted this way since Josiah's death, the Lord would remove David's lineage from the throne. His house would be left desolate, at least until a worthy heir emerged. Apparently some persons hoped that Jehoahaz (Shallum), a king deposed in 609 B.C., would return to Jerusalem to reign, but their hopes were not to materialize. Like Zedekiah's wishes, such dreams were the fantasies of a disobedient people wanting to be released from the consequences of their actions.

Wicked Kings Have Led the Nation to Destruction (22:13–30)

Now the text denounces Jehoiakim, who ruled from 609–598 B.C. This unworthy replacement for Josiah was placed in power by Egypt, and he managed to change loyalties to Babylon when it became necessary to do so. Indeed, his only consistent loyalty was not to Judah's people but to himself. As the book unfolds, it becomes abundantly clear that he had no use for Jeremiah and his meddlesome messages.

Jeremiah complained that Jehoiakim believed that what made him a good king was the amount of wealth he could accumulate. He built a new palace while his citizens were lacking life's necessities. All the while he shed the blood of innocent persons and oppressed the poor to get what he wanted. For these actions he would die, but no one would mourn his passing. Instead his death would have no more mourners than a donkey would at its death. Similarly, the nation and its former kings would die as well. Sadly, the nation was no more faithful to God's covenant standards than their kings had been.

A Righteous King Is Coming (23:1–8)

Despite this succession of unjust, cowardly, and self-centered rulers, the Lord was not finished with the house of David. After all, God promised David an eternal kingdom (2 Sam. 7:1–17). Therefore, the Lord pronounced woe on these wretched "shepherds" who were leading Judah to destruction. Kings like Jehoiakim and Zedekiah richly deserved divine censure. But in the future God would raise a righteous King from David's line. This individual would be wise, just, and righteous. He would save the people and cause them to dwell securely in the land. His rule would mark the end of Israel's long exile from their God. Without question, this figure was the Messiah, the Christ, the one whom the New Testament claims is Jesus. Only Christ could redeem the sinful people and the fallen house of David.

"But now God has shown us a different way of being right in his sight—not by obeying the law but by the way promised in the Scriptures long ago. We are made right in God's sight when we trust in Jesus Christ to take away our sins. And we can all be saved in this same way, no matter who we are or what we have done" (Rom. 3:21–22, NLT).

- *The nation was sinful, and had suffered at*
- *the hands of unjust rulers. God would punish*
- *both ruler and people by sending the Babylo-*
- *nians to devastate the land. In the future,*
- *however, God would send a righteous king*
- *who will save the chosen nation from its sins.*

JEREMIAH OPPOSES THE FALSE PROPHETS (23:9–40)

Having opposed the kings, Jeremiah now directed his messages at prophets who did not tell Judah the truth about their sins and the consequences of those sins. These prophets preached for monetary gain. They were polluted, immoral, and worthy of judgment. They preached whatever fit their agenda, not the words the Lord would have the people hear. Such worthless "ministers" were leading an already rebellious nation into further covenant breaking. Therefore, God would send them out of the land with the corrupt monarchs denounced in 21:1–23:8.

- *God's prophets preach the truth, however*
- *painful the truth may be.*

JEREMIAH OPPOSES THE PEOPLE (24:1–25:38)

Although the people had not had good spiritual or political leaders, they remained responsible for their own actions. Part of the reason the leaders had been so terrible was that the nation would not tolerate God-honoring kings, priests, and prophets. Just look how they treated

Jeremiah! This section charts Judah's early descent and warns that even worse times are ahead.

The People Are Like Good and Bad Figs (24:1–10)

This passage refers to the time about 605 B.C., when Babylon first gained control over Judah. At this time the Babylonians took several Judaites captive, including such promising young leaders as Daniel, Shadrach, Meshach, and Abednego. Certainly, this exile was a terrible disappointment to the nation, but it was just the beginning of their woes.

Jeremiah was given a vision of two baskets of figs, one good and one bad. God declared that the good figs, the ones God favored, were the Jews who had gone to Babylon. The bad figs that the Lord condemned were the Judaites who remained in the Promised Land. God promised to bless the exiles, but those who stayed in Judah and sinned against the Lord would suffer worse punishment than those who had gone into exile. God would give the exiles a heart to serve Him, but would turn the other figs over to destruction.

The People Will Be Exiled Seventy Years (25:1–14)

This message was given about 605 B.C., which is the same general time frame as the preceding text. Jeremiah stated that he had been preaching God's word for twenty-three years, yet the nation had paid no attention. Now they were in desperate trouble. Babylon had exiled a number of the populace, and more telling defeats were to come. Indeed, the Babylonians would destroy Judah and take the rest of the people into exile. There they would stay for seventy years.

The book of Daniel indicates that God kept this promise to the captives in Babylon, for the Lord protected Daniel and his friends. "In the first year of his reign, I, Daniel, understood from the Scriptures, according to the word of the LORD given to Jeremiah the prophet, that the desolation of Jerusalem would last seventy years. So I turned to the Lord God and pleaded with him in prayer and petition, in fasting, and in sackcloth and ashes. I prayed to the LORD my God and confessed: 'O Lord, the great and awesome God, who keeps his covenant of love with all who love him and obey his commands, we have sinned and done wrong. We have been wicked and rebelled; we have turned away from your commands and laws'" (Dan. 9:2–5).

Neglecting the Lord's commands to forsake the worship of other gods was leading them to increasing disaster.

These predictions come true in 587 B.C. when Babylon conquered the land and destroyed Jerusalem. It was not until about 538–535 B.C. that Jewish refugees were allowed to return to their homeland. Dating from about 605 B.C., then, the frame was almost exactly seventy years. God's word comes true even in small details, as Judah would discover, much to their dismay.

God's Wrath Will Be Poured Out on Many Nations (25:15–38)

Israel would not be alone in their experience of God's wrath. Small and great countries alike would fall to the Babylonians, whom the Lord had chosen to be the instrument of His judgment. This judgment would be as thorough as it would be horrible. Disaster would spread from one nation to the next, for sin had spread throughout God's created world. God, who made the heavens and the earth, would punish all the wicked.

JEREMIAH OPPOSES FALSE WORSHIP AND FALSE PROPHECY (26:1–29:32)

This section strikes at the source of Judah's spiritual and moral problems: their priests and prophets. These groups have been addressed before, but they are placed under even greater scrutiny here. They responded with vigorous opposition of their own. At every turn they attempted to gain public support at Jeremiah's expense. In doing so they reinforced the people in their sins and made divine judgment inevitable.

The Lord Will Destroy the Temple (26:6)

As in 7:15, Jeremiah preached against the pseudo worship at the Temple. His intent was to point out the people's faults so the current Temple would not become as desolate as Shiloh, one of the early homes of the ark of the covenant. What he discovered, however, was that the nation had come to believe that the sheer presence of a physical Temple assured God's favor. Thus, they considered Jeremiah a heretic for suggesting that the Temple could be destroyed.

The Priests and Prophets Denounce Jeremiah (26:7–15)

God had sent Jeremiah, but the prophets and priests did not accept his message. Indeed, this failure to listen to God-sent individuals was one of the nation's biggest problems. Why listen to an unpleasant message when other so-called religious leaders said kinder things? The leaders' displeasure with Jeremiah caused them to call for his execution. Once again Jeremiah risked his life for the Lord's work.

Jeremiah Is Spared Death (26:16–24)

In an unexpected scenario, Jeremiah was spared death when the elders of the land remembered the truthful, though negative, words Micah had spoken against Jerusalem one hundred years earlier (Mic. 3:12). At that time the nation listened and repented. Oddly, though the elders cited this previous episode, no repentance resulted from this exchange. They noted the validity of Jeremiah's right to preach as he had done, but they did not grant the validity of his message.

Several times Jeremiah denounced false prophets. In the ancient world, most religions had their own prophets and priests. In many countries the prophets had the responsibility of interpreting the future, often through the use of sorcery or the reading of animal entrails. In Israel, false prophets were persons who led the people to worship gods other than the Lord, or who preached messages from their own heads rather than from the Lord.

"'They will fight against you but will not overcome you, for I am with you and will rescue you,' declares the Lord" (Jer. 1:19).

The People Must Reject False Prophecy Concerning Babylon (27:1–22)

At the beginning of Zedekiah's reign (c. 597 B.C.), the Lord stated that Babylon would indeed conquer Judah. Therefore, the Lord commanded Judah to serve the one he had chosen to rule over them. False prophets claimed that not only would Babylon not conquer Jerusalem, but they also declared that those items taken previously by Babylon would be returned. Clearly, they told the people that Babylon's power would wane. Jeremiah warned the people not to heed such fantasies. Renewal would occur only after exile.

The People Must Reject False Prophecy about Exile (28:1–17)

That same year Jeremiah encountered a specific false prophet named Hananiah. This prophet declared that within two years Babylon's power would cease. The vessels taken from the Temple would be returned, the exiles would come home, and the deposed king would come home. Clearly, Jeremiah wished Hananiah was right, but he knew that he was not. The Lord had determined that Israel's time for repentance had expired. Indeed, He knew that the nation had no intention of repenting. Therefore, the end was nearer than the people thought.

After an initial encounter, Jeremiah told Hananiah that Babylon's grip on Judah was like iron. There was no chance that Israel would escape. Further, Hananiah would die for his misleading words to the people. Just as Jeremiah promised, Hananiah died, which indicated which of the two men actually had a word from the Lord. Sadly, the Israelites did not listen to Jeremiah even then. They rejected the admonition to forsake false prophets.

The People Must Reject False Prophecy about the Return from Exile (29:1–32)

Judah suffered "mini-exiles" in 605 and 597 B.C. before the great Exile of 587 B.C. In this passage Jeremiah wrote a letter to the Jewish people who had preceded their countrymen in exile. They had been hearing from false prophets that the exile would end soon and that they would be able to return to their homeland. Again, Jeremiah could only wish that they were correct.

Unfortunately, the Exile would last seventy years. Therefore, the exiles should build homes, plant vineyards, and generally prepare to stay until they died. They would not be coming home. Still, the Lord loved them. As they turned to God, they could be certain that the Lord would respond to them. What distinguished them from their brothers and sisters remaining in Judah was this willingness to seek the Lord. As they believed in God where they lived, they would fare much better than those who remained in Judah and rebelled against the Lord. If they refused to heed false prophecy, God would bless them, even in exile.

Israel first began to return to the land in 538–535 B.C., when Cyrus the Great allowed them to come home. Times were hard for those who led the return. Ezra and Nehemiah found Jerusalem still in ruins as late as 450 B.C.

■ *True prophecy agrees with God's written*
■ *word and is inspired by the Lord. False*
■ *prophecy is based on human wishes and*
■ *human unwillingness to turn to the Lord and*
■ *the Lord's will. Those who are pleasing to*
■ *God accept God's will, respond to God's*
■ *word, and refuse to listen to lying prophets.*

QUESTIONS TO GUIDE YOUR STUDY

1. How many years did Jeremiah prophesy? How many kings ruled during this period?
2. How can we tell that Zedekiah wasn't hearing anything Jeremiah was saying?
3. Explain the meaning of the vision of the figs in the fig basket.
4. What did Jeremiah tell those already in exile to do?

THE GOD WHO OFFERS RESTORATION AND THE NEW COVENANT (CHAPS. 30–33)

After twenty-nine chapters of nearly unrelenting negative preaching, the prophet at last turned to more positive themes. These positive messages clearly stated that the good news only pertained to the future. Still, Jeremiah was allowed to preach hope and joy. While doing so, he offered some of the most significant theological statements in the Old Testament. Indeed, the whole notion of a New Covenant, or a New Testament, arises from this section of the book. Just as the previous chapters denounced the nation, the people, and the leaders, so this section emphasizes the renewal of each.

GOD WILL RESTORE THE NATION (30:1–24)

God had made it clear that Judah's sins would be punished by an invasion of a foreign army. This army would destroy every vestige of their national religious, cultural, and political heritage. Exile awaited a disobedient people of God. But exile is not God's final word concerning Israel. Days were coming when the Lord would restore that which Babylon would ruin. Slowly, with great thoroughness, the prophet described a complete restoration.

Hope Will Replace Fear and Despair (30:1–11)

Because of the promised invasion and loss of land and people, Israel had plenty of reason to be afraid. Now, however, they could look forward to a time of restored fortunes, of freedom from bondage, of restoration of their kingdom.

God would bring them back to their homeland, would protect them from harm, and would place David's heir on the throne. Despair would turn to confidence in the Lord because the Lord would be with Israel. God's presence would guarantee victory, peace, and hope.

Wounds Will Be Healed (30:12–17)

After the Lord had punished Israel justly, God would drive the elect nation's enemies away. Their wounds had been significant, but their healing would be even greater. Their "lovers," their foreign gods, had led to their defeat by foreign nations. They had thereby become a sick and demoralized people, but God would heal all their national illnesses by dismissing all their enemies. Clearly, the just God was also a forgiving and saving God.

Building Will Replace Destruction (30:18–24)

With the populace restored to the land and their foes driven out, the Lord would proceed to help the Israelites rebuild Jerusalem and the country's other cities. In this way all the physical parts of the nation would be back in place. The holy people would once again dwell in the Holy Land and have the holy city for their capital. All that Israel had done in the past would be fully punished, and all that Israel could be in the future would become possible.

These promises began to be fulfilled when the Temple was rebuilt in 520–516 B.C. through the preaching of Haggai and Zechariah and through the leadership of Zerubbabel. By Jesus' era the land had been restored, a beautiful Temple was in place, and the land had rest from war. Everything was in place for spiritual renewal.

■ *God would not fail to punish Israel, but pun-*
■ *ishment was sent to effect repentance and for-*
■ *giveness. The Lord would restore everything*
■ *lost in the time of punishment. Divine forgive-*
■ *ness more than cancels divine chastisement.*

GOD WILL MAKE A NEW COVENANT WITH ISRAEL (31:1–40)

Throughout the Old Testament, the Lord made covenants with individuals and with Israel. The word *covenant* originally meant "bond" or "fetter," and came to mean, "binding relationship." Covenants in the Old Testament were made between a greater (God) and a lesser (an individual or Israel), and required the lesser to obey the greater. In return, the greater promised to help and bless the lesser. Therefore, covenants were binding relationships between God and an individual or God and Israel in which God offered blessing and Israel or an individual pledged allegiance to God.

Although other covenants appear in the Old Testament, there are three major covenants that deserve attention. First, the Lord promised to give Abraham heirs, a great name, a homeland, fame, and protection, and He also pledged that all nations would be blessed through Abraham (Gen. 12:19). This covenant was made to last forever (Gen. 17:7).

Second, the Lord made a covenant with Israel at Mount Sinai that was mediated through Moses (Exod. 20; Lev. 27). At this time the Lord pledged to bless Israel, and Israel pledged to follow God's commands and requirements for the securing of forgiveness of sins. At no time does the text call the Mosaic Covenant eternal. There would come a time when laws would no longer be needed because sin would no longer be a problem. Third, God promised David an eternal kingdom (2 Sam. 7:11). Obviously, this covenant, like the Abrahamic covenant, must endure forever. The Old Testament texts that focus on a coming king, or Messiah, all look to David's family for the fulfillment of this promise (cp. Jer. 23:18).

Thus, when God promised a New Covenant in Jeremiah 31:31–34, this New Covenant must not negate the eternal covenants. In fact, it must participate with them. It is possible that a New Covenant could supercede the Mosaic Covenant, but this possibility is not adopted in these verses. What is clear is that this covenant is part of God's plan to restore the people, the leaders, and the land. It is also evident that it is a future promise from Jeremiah's historical perspective.

Israel Will Be God's People (31:1–14)

Though never disowned by God, the nation had certainly been acting as if they were not the Lord's people. After all, they had worshiped other deities and broken God's law. With punishment over, though, the Lord would once again forge a faithful group of servants. God's love would lead to the return of refugees to the land, to renewed worship in Zion, and to the emergence of responsible religious leaders. God's direct action would make certain that these benefits occurred.

God Will Have Mercy on Weary Israel (31:15–26)

Israel's time in exile had led to great weeping. The people had grown weary and disheartened in their distressing circumstances. To their credit, a remnant of believers had repented of their sins and had returned to the living God. Therefore, God considered Israel a delightful child, one for whom God's heart yearned. The Israelites would come home. Their cities would be inhabited, and their end would be better than their beginning. God's love would energize

God said to Abraham, "I will establish my covenant as an everlasting covenant between me and you and your descendants after you for the generations to come, to be your God and the God of your descendants after you" (Gen. 17:7).

Through Nathan, the prophet, the Lord told David, "Your house and your kingdom will endure forever before me; your throne will be established forever" (2 Sam. 7:16).

the broken sinners; God's grace would make them pure again.

God Will Watch Over the People to Make Them Secure (31:27–30)

In days to come the Lord would be as careful to bless Israel as he had been to punish them. They must understand, though, that this new kindness did not mean they could act however they wished and suffer no consequences. God would make certain that each person who sinned would be held accountable for his or her actions.

God Will Make a New Covenant with Israel (31:31–40)

Most importantly, in the future the Lord would make a New Covenant with Israel. This covenant would differ from the old covenant, which surely means the Mosaic Covenant here, in specific ways. First, it would not be broken as the Mosaic Covenant was. The problem was not with the Law itself, but with unfaithful Israel, who repeatedly rejected the Lord's commands because of lack of faith and a rebellious heart.

Second, God would place this law directly on the people's hearts. The law was always an internalized, heart-oriented covenant, but the nation turned its heart away from God. Such rebellion would not be possible in the New Covenant, for God would implant obedience into their lives.

Third, the New Covenant people will know the Lord. In old Israel some of the chosen nation loved and knew the Lord, while most rejected God's love. In the New Covenant community, all the covenant partners would know and love the Lord. There would no longer be a remnant of believers within a generally wicked nation.

Only believers would be counted as God's people. Only believers would constitute Israel.

Fourth, this New Covenant would be eternal. In this way it would mesh with the Abrahamic and Davidic covenants. It would last as long as creation existed, and it would guarantee that Zion would always be the special city of the Lord.

This New Covenant is fulfilled in Christ and the church. Christ is the heir of David who rules forever and the means by which Abraham blesses the nations. The church consists of persons from all nations who know the Lord. Each one will live forever in the new Zion, which is commonly referred to as heaven. In other words, the New Covenant keeps continuity with the older covenants, yet advances God's will at the same time.

- *God always punishes to restore. In this pas-*
- *sage, God will restore in a manner that lasts*
- *forever. By making a New Covenant with*
- *those who believe in Him, God provides a*
- *way of salvation that creates a faithful group*
- *of worshipers.*

GOD WILL BRING ISRAEL BACK TO THE PROMISED LAND (32:1–44)

After the lofty promises of chapters 30 and 31, Jeremiah 32 brings the account back to earth. It was fine to speak of future restoration, but the harsh historical reality for Jeremiah was that he and his contemporaries must live through the punishment that would produce the renewal. As in earlier chapters, the Lord commanded Jeremiah to complete a symbolic act that would address the people's spiritual needs. This act

Zion

The transliteration of the Hebrew and Greek words that originally referred to the fortified hill of pre-Israelite Jersualem between the Kedron and Typopean valleys. Scholars disagree as to the root meaning of the term. Some authorities have suggested that the word was related to the Hebrew word that meant "dry place" or "parched ground." Others relate the word to an Arabic term that is interpreted as "hillcrest," or "mountainous ridge." The name *Zion* was mentioned first in the account of David's conquest of Jerusalem (2 Sam. 5:6–10; 1 Chron. 11:4–9).

had the prophet buying land just before the Babylonians controlled Judah, an act that was ludicrous unless there was some long-term future for Israel. Indeed, this symbolic deed proclaimed to the nation that they would some day return to the land. The book has already stated that the Exile would last seventy years, but no longer, so this passage reinforced that previous assurance.

The Command to Buy Land (32:1–15)

During Babylon's final siege of Jerusalem, or about 588–587 B.C., God told Jeremiah to engage in what must have seemed to him the strangest symbolic act of all. With land all but worthless because of the certain fall of the city, God told the prophet to buy some property. Of course, the prospective seller was eager to do business. This transaction made Jeremiah look foolish in the eyes of his countrymen once more. Although it was a sound long-term investment, it did not seem so at the moment.

A Serious Question and a Firm Response (32:16–35)

Despite his willingness to obey the Lord's odd command, the prophet asked for an explanation of the Lord's orders. Certainly God is great enough to do all things, even bring the people back to the land. But what puzzled Jeremiah was that he had preached judgment as God commanded, yet now he was to act as if the invasion would not come off after all. Why buy land if the invasion would succeed?

God answered by repeating His charges against Israel. The people had sinned, and they would suffer the loss of the land. This symbolic act was not meant to negate all that Jeremiah had preached thus far. Rather, it was to give notice of God's intent to restore the people back to their homeland. God would make certain that exile was not the end of the chosen ones.

God Will Bring the Exiles Home (32:36–44)

To prove that "nothing is impossible with God," the Lord would bring the people back to the land. Then, the Lord would be their God, and they would be His people. God would give them new hearts and an everlasting covenant. God would bring as much good to them as He had brought punishment, and at that time, land would be bought and sold again.

We may be called on by the Lord to obey Him in ways that we may not understand at the time. The command may be based on Scripture, but the timing and circumstances may appear strange to us. We need to obey. In time we will see why God has called us to a task. Often, the answer to our questions comes soon after we are obedient.

Clearly, these promises connect this text to Jeremiah 31:31–40. In both places God pledged a new and permanent covenant, and in each text full restoration of land, people, and worship was predicted. Forgiveness will be as thorough as judgment. These benefits would emerge because of the Lord's work on Israel's behalf, not as a result of Israel's goodness.

- *Nothing is impossible with God, not even for-*
- *giving gross sinners. Nothing is impossible*
- *with God, not even restoring an exiled people*
- *to their land. Nothing is impossible with*
- *God, not even the ability to show wrath and*
- *love in equally appropriate measures.*

GOD KEEPS HIS PROMISES (33:1–26)

God had made wonderful long-term promises to Israel. They could look forward to a future brighter than their present. Throughout their history, though, Israel had failed to trust the Lord's word, for they had refused to believe that God is trustworthy. Therefore, this chapter focuses on God's character. It emphasizes that

"Because God wanted to make the unchanging nature of his purpose very clear to the heirs of what was promised, he confirmed it with an oath. God did this so that, by two unchangeable things in which it is impossible for God to lie, we who have fled to take hold of the hope offered to us may be greatly encouraged" (Heb. 6:17–18).

the God who promises is the God who keeps His promises. God's nature guarantees the truthfulness of His statements.

The Lord Promises to Direct the Future (33:1–5)

During the Babylonian's siege of Jerusalem, Jeremiah was held prisoner for proclaiming that the enemy would overrun the city. While he was in prison, the Lord spoke to him, reminding the prophet that God is the maker of heaven and earth, which means that God is able to do whatever is necessary to make His promises come true. Also, as the maker of all things, including time, the Lord is able to predict the future, and the immediate future will not be pleasant.

The Lord Promises to Heal (33:6–13)

Next, Jeremiah heard that the Creator is also a healer. God gave His word that Israel's sins would be forgiven and that they would enjoy peace and prosperity. Besides the people themselves, the Lord would heal the land. It would once again be inhabited and become fertile. Because of this healing, the nation would respond with worship, praise, and thanksgiving. As Ruler of all things, God would fulfill these promises.

The Lord Promises to Honor the Davidic Covenant (33:14–26)

Finally, the Lord claimed to be one who keeps covenant commitments. In particular, all pledges made to David will be kept. The eternal covenant cannot be broken. David will have an heir on the throne forever, just as was promised in 2 Samuel 7:1–17. As long as the created order exists, the Lord will keep this covenant. The messianic hope is as certain as the character of God Himself.

■ *The fidelity of God's Word is grounded in the*
■ *completeness of God's person. As Creator,*
■ *Healer, Ruler, and Covenant Keeper, the*
■ *Lord deserves to be trusted. God can do all*
■ *good things, but He cannot lie.*

QUESTIONS TO GUIDE YOUR STUDY

1. What did Jeremiah prophesy would happen beyond the destruction of Judah and the Exile?
2. When was this prophecy fulfilled?
3. Compare the New Covenant with the covenant given at Sinai.
4. During the siege of Jerusalem, what did the Lord command Jeremiah to do? What was the meaning of this command?

THE GOD WHO JUDGES ISRAEL AND THE NATIONS (CHAPS. 34–51)

The Lord had threatened judgment, sent some Israelites into captivity, and given the people time to repent. In every way, the Lord had been faithful and patient. Now, however, the time for patience and benevolence had expired. Babylon had taken Judah's land. But the text does not stop with God's punishing of the elect nation. As the Creator of the universe, God has the right and responsibility to assess the behavior of all peoples everywhere. Thus, God exerts sovereignty over all countries in this section. By conveying the Lord's word to these nations, Jeremiah fulfilled his calling to be a prophet to the nations (1:4–10).

GOD'S FAITHFULNESS AND ISRAEL'S INFIDELITY (34:1–35:19)

God's truthfulness had been firmly established in the preceding chapters. This fidelity stands in stark contrast to Israel's behavior in chapters 34–35. Here the nation breaks covenant with one another and with the God who chose, delivered, and loved them. They proved as unfaithful as God proved faithful. Only a small remnant of believers like Jeremiah and other persons who appear in the next few chapters remained committed to their vows to the Lord. Such behavior can only result in divine judgment.

God Is Faithful to the Davidic Covenant (34:1–17)

As the Babylonians came closer and closer to taking Jerusalem, the king implored Jeremiah to give him a hopeful message from the Lord.

Sadly, no such encouragement would be given to one so unwilling to take the hard road of repentance. Despite the monarch's moral weakness, God promised that the king would not be killed in the invasion. David's lineage would survive, albeit in exile. The eternal covenant would be obscured for a time, yet never would be revoked.

Israel Is Unfaithful to One Another (34:18–22)

The Mosaic Law allowed voluntary servitude for seven years. Obviously, this arrangement would not be needed unless the one volunteering was in financial distress. At the end of this time, servants decided whether to remain with their masters. In any case, servants of Israelite or foreign descent were to be set free during jubilee years (cp. Exod. 21:2–11; Lev. 25:10–55). The whole system was intended to provide mercy for hurting people. During the Babylonian invasion, the Israelites set their servants free. When the immediate threat passed, however, they enslaved their countrymen. This lack of compassion for others and lack of obedience to God was all too typical. The nation was "faithful" only when it was convenient. Their hypocrisy was evident, and their punishment was inevitable.

Israel Is Unfaithful to Their Heavenly Father (35:1–19)

Once more the Lord used an object lesson to proclaim the nature of Israel's transgressions. This time Jeremiah interviewed a family that had been committed to their patriarch's commands for generations. They were scrupulous in their observance of clan traditions, and in their commitment to the Lord. In stark contrast, Israel had been redeemed from Egypt, given the

Promised Land, entrusted with the prophets' divinely-inspired messages, and been privileged to hear God's warnings when they had erred, but they had rejected their God's commands. Disobedience of this sort would not be tolerated in an earthly family, and neither would it be countenanced by the Lord.

■ By any reasonable standard, the Israelites
■ merited condemnation. Their unfaithfulness
■ and unwillingness to repent in the face of
■ God's goodness and fidelity marked them as
■ ungrateful and grossly oblivious to right and
■ wrong.

ISRAEL HAS REJECTED GOD'S WRITTEN AND SPOKEN WORD (36:1–32)

Already the book has recounted numerous occasions on which Israel refused to listen to Jeremiah's warnings and admonitions. At no time did large numbers of the people admit the truthfulness of his statements or the compassion with which they were offered. Of all the callous rejections of his words, however, the one in this account may be the worst. Here the prophet's words, which were God's words, were burned like trash.

God's Merciful Revelation of the Truth (36:1–19)

God's revealed word is always initiated in love. It is always issued in mercy and grace directed toward persons who cannot save or reform themselves. In Jehoiakim's fifth year (about 605 B.C.), the Lord sent Jeremiah to preach to the people and their leaders. Because he was restricted from going to the

Temple (perhaps because of his messages in chaps. 7 and 26), he dictated his sermon to his scribe/friend Baruch and asked him to read it at the house of the Lord. God's wrath was burning against the nation, but he was willing to forgive if they would repent. The message was so powerful that the Temple officials took the book to the king.

Jehoiakim's Callous Treatment of God's Word (36:20–26)

When the king heard the scroll read to him, he did not repent. He did not even wonder if Jeremiah was correct. Rather, he cut it up and tossed it on the fire. Thus, he denied the truthfulness of God's message, the validity of God's messenger, and the applicability of God's word for his life. Without hesitation, he rejected God's merciful revelation and opened Himself to God's wrath.

God's Indomitable Word (36:27–32)

Although the scroll had been burned, God's word was not silenced. Indeed, nothing can stifle the Word of the Lord. Jeremiah was told to dictate another scroll, and he did so. At its writing the Lord promised that Babylon would conquer Judah. This event was eighteen years away, but it would come as certainly as the worlds came into existence at the issuing of God's word. Jehoiakim would pass away, but God's word would not.

"He answered, 'Then I beg you, father, send Lazarus to my father's house, for I have five brothers. Let him warn them, so that they will not also come to this place of torment.' "Abraham replied, 'They have Moses and the Prophets; let them listen to them.' "'No, father Abraham,' he said, 'but if someone from the dead goes to them, they will repent.' "He said to him, 'If they do not listen to Moses and the Prophets, they will not be convinced even if someone rises from the dead'" (Luke 16:27–31).

- God's Word is alive and powerful. It is
- offered by grace by a loving Creator. Those
- who reject it separate themselves from the
- God who sends it.

JERUSALEM'S LAST DAYS (37:1–39:18)

Having ignored God's written and spoken word, the nation had left itself with no hope of avoiding the inevitable, cataclysmic Babylonian invasion. Even as Babylon's armies surrounded Jerusalem, the kings and people refused to accept Jeremiah's words as accurate or final. Instead, they accused him of treason and treachery, ironic claims for persons who plotted and schemed against the prophet.

Jeremiah Warns Against Self-Deception (37:1–10)

Judah's last king, Zedekiah (c. 597–587 B.C.), wavered between seeking advice from Jeremiah and fearing the people. He did not take Jeremiah's advice, yet he asked the prophet to pray for the nation's deliverance. When Babylon temporarily withdrew from Jerusalem, the king apparently thought the worst was over. Perhaps Jeremiah had been wrong after all. Jeremiah told him not to deceive himself. God's will had already been revealed: Judah would fall to Babylon. To believe anything else was to place the nation in a worse position.

Jeremiah Is Imprisoned (37:11–21)

The nation's anger at Jeremiah finally exploded. When he left the city to check on some land, he was falsely accused of deserting to the Babylonians. Despite his protestations, he was jailed. The king asked him what God said about the future, and once again Jeremiah told him the sad truth. Whether in jail or in freedom, the prophet kept faith with the people and with the word of God. He never wavered from the truth, though it cost him dearly.

Jeremiah Is Delivered (38:1–16)

Things grew worse for the prophet. Since he knew that Jerusalem would be destroyed, he counseled the people to surrender to the Babylonians. For this "treason," he was dropped in a muddy cistern, where he suffered greatly. His only crime was telling the truth to a people in peril.

But Jeremiah was delivered from the cistern by Ebed-Melech, an Ethiopian serving in Zedekiah's court. Believing Jeremiah the victim of wicked men, Ebed-Melech boldly petitioned the king on Jeremiah's behalf. The king agreed that the prophet should be released. Later the king asked a word from God, and heard Jeremiah proclaim the same, old message. Israel might as well surrender, for God would not save them from their foe.

Jeremiah Presents Zedekiah's Options (38:17–28)

Unbelievably, Zedekiah asked Jeremiah for counsel yet another time. It was as if he simply hoped against hope that God had changed His mind for no reason, or for some reason Zedekiah could not fathom. Jeremiah presented him with two stark options: he could surrender and the city would survive under Babylonian control, or he could resist and have the people killed and the city burned. Sadly, Zedekiah feared the people more than he feared the Lord. He believed he would be murdered if he took the prophet's advice. Political expediency had become so grounded in his character that he was impotent in the face of a difficult decision. He made no commitment to doing what Jeremiah advised.

"How deserted lies the city,
once so full of people!
How like a widow is she,
who once was great among the nations!
She who was queen among the provinces
has now become a slave.
Bitterly she weeps at night,
tears are upon her cheeks.
Among all her lovers there is none to comfort her.
All her friends have betrayed her;
they have become her enemies.
After affliction and harsh labor,
Judah has gone into exile.
She dwells among the nations;
she finds no resting place.
All who pursue her have overtaken her
in the midst of her distress" (Lam. 1:1–3).

Jerusalem Is Destroyed (39:1–10)

Finally the terrible day arrived. In an amazingly brief text, the book states that the city fell in 587 B.C. When the Babylonians breached the wall, the king tried to flee, but to no avail. He was captured. The Babylonians killed his sons in his sight, then took his sight away. Blinded, he was taken into exile, a broken and disgraced former monarch. Like their king, the people who rejected Jeremiah's warnings fell victim to the very thing he predicted.

Israel had lost the land promised to Abraham, conquered by Joshua, and governed by David. Solomon's Temple, the very one the nation believed was a symbol of eternal national security, was destroyed. The holy people had lost their holy status, their holy place, and their Holy Land. Perhaps no event in Israelite history had a more devastating impact on the nation's history. It would be more than four hundred years before the Jews would rule themselves again.

God Delivers Jeremiah and Ebed-Melech (39:11–18)

From the start the Lord had promised Jeremiah that he would not be killed by his enemies (1:17–19), and God had kept that promise. God also spared the life of the Ethiopian Ebed-Melech. Both faithful men learned that the Lord protects those who trust in Him. Faith was the only means of victory in the difficult days during which they lived.

- *God's Word comes true no matter what*
- *world events seem to imply. Those who reject*
- *that Word have cut themselves off from the*
- *human race's only source of hope. At the*
- *same time, even in the midst of the most dan-*
- *gerous times, the Lord is able and willing to*
- *protect those who trust in Him.*

JUDAH'S REMNANT REBELS AGAINST BABYLON (40:1–41:18)

As if their problems were not great enough already, the Jews who remained in and near Jerusalem rebelled against the Babylonians. This decision required them to commit murder, to protect the killers, and to consider leaving the land to go to Egypt. As Zedekiah had done, they asked for God's word from Jeremiah. Like Zedekiah, they refused to believe and obey that Word when it came. They compounded their previous sins with stupidity.

It is important to accept the conditions of punishment from God. Instead of serving the nation the Lord used to punish them, the Jews continued to fight against God's will. In contrast, Moses accepted his role even after he learned he would not go into the Promised Land. Our faithfulness may be most impressive when it is offered even though we may not be getting exactly what we want.

Jeremiah Is Freed (40:1–16)

Ironically, Jeremiah had to be freed by the Babylonians rather than his own people. The Babylonians probably appreciated his predictions about their inevitable success. Still, it is sad that the prophet's own nation could not have seen the truth of his statements and kept him free from imprisonment.

Jeremiah chose to remain among his own people rather than to go to Babylon with the conquerors. Apparently he believed he would have no right to preach about their renewal unless he shared in their suffering. He also stated in chapters 32–33 that the Lord would restore the nation to the land in days to come, so he continued in the land in that hope.

The Plot Against Babylon's Appointed Governor (41:1–10)

Babylon appointed Gedaliah governor over what remained of the population. He encouraged the people to harvest their crops and to make the land fruitful. His strategy for ruling the remaining Jews was to make them happy so they would serve Babylon willingly, an attitude that would have the added benefit of keeping Babylon out of the Jews' business.

Unfortunately, a plot against Gedaliah was pursued. Ishmael murdered him, and then took hostages and killed other citizens. Ishmael's plan was to flee to Ammon, thereby leaving the Jews around Jerusalem to deal with the Babylonians' wrath. Clearly, this rebellion could only make an already terrible situation worse.

The Hostages Are Rescued (41:11–18)

An Israelite commander named Johanan came to the hostages' rescue. He freed the captives and drove Ishmael into Ammon, stripped of all support except for eight men. The people now faced the problem of dealing with the Babylonians. One possibility was for them to flee to Egypt, a country that opposed Babylon. The other possibility was to stay and accept whatever consequences came their way.

- ■ *Even a bad situation can be made worse by*
- ■ *poor judgment and sinful behavior. Rectify-*
- ■ *ing an error often necessitates important*
- ■ *decisions about the future.*

JUDAH'S REMNANT REBELS AGAINST GOD (42:1–45:5)

Now the people faced a crucial decision. Would they stay in the land or flee? How would they remain safe? To help them decide, they sought a divine word from the Lord. For that word they turned to Jeremiah, whose accuracy by now was unquestioned. The fact that they did not believe Jeremiah even now indicates the depth of their rebellion against the Lord. New disobedience will require new punishment. As always, only those who are faithful can expect the Lord's protection, and in this account only Jeremiah and Baruch were faithful.

The word *remnant* means the minority in Israel that had faith in God and kept their covenant with Him. Historically, the faithful were rarely a large percentage of the nature, Still, it was this small number that the Lord used to write the Bible, preach the Word, and maintain proper Temple worship. Christians today must be faithful even if they are in the minority.

The People Request a Word from God (42:1–6)

Being desperate, the people asked the prophet for God's word on their predicament. They swore they would do what God said, whether it was unpleasant or pleasant. They appeared to have learned from all the previous times they did not listen to Jeremiah.

Jeremiah Delivers God's Word (42:7–22)

After ten days the Lord's word came to the prophet. He declared that the people should stay in the land and promised that if they did, the Lord would bless them greatly. They could be sure that the Lord would protect them, prosper them, and guide them. On the other hand, if they rebelled and fled to Egypt, they would suffer and die, for the Babylonians were going to ravage Egypt—the exact fate they feared would overtake them if they tried to leave their homeland. Their choice was clear. God had spoken, and had spoken compassionately.

The People Reject God's Word (43:1–7)

Just as Jeremiah suspected in 42:21–22, those seeking the word from God had no intention of doing what God said. Rather, they accused Jeremiah and Baruch of wanting to hand them over to the Babylonians so they could be sent into exile. This far-fetched reasoning masked their deep-seated devotion to following their own chosen path. Not content to flee to Egypt themselves, they also forced Jeremiah and Baruch to go with them. It was as if they thought the pair was some sort of protection against God, the Babylonians, or both. But they had actually guaranteed that they would endure terrible suffering and face certain death.

God's Rejection of the People (43:8–13)

God instructed Jeremiah to perform one last symbolic act. The prophet was to take some stones and place them in a specific location. Then he declared that the king of Babylon would place his throne over these very stones. In other words, Babylon would conquer Egypt just as they had overrun Judah. Leaving the Land of Promise had once more given them into the hands of the people God had chosen to punish the wicked. This instrument of wrath would devastate all those who worship idols, as well as the idols themselves. The Lord alone is God; no other so-called deity may be recognized on judgment day.

God's Rejection of Idolatry (44:1–14)

Jeremiah did not stop preaching even though he had been forced into exile in Egypt. He continued to be faithful to his calling to the very end of his life. Now he explained the main currents of Israelite history in a manner similar to other biblical texts (see 2 Kings 17). He stated that Israel's breaking of the first two Commandments led the Lord to send prophets to warn of coming punishment. Despite this offer of grace, they persisted in their sins, thus ensuring their national demise. Their most recent rejection of God's word was just one more in a long series of rebellions against God and the covenant they made with Him. They chose idolatry even now, which means they chose death.

The People Confess Love for Idols (44:15–19)

Having heard this message, the people were not contrite and penitent. In fact, they reacted indignantly. They argued that their main problem was that they had not served other gods faithfully enough! When their families were committed to star gods, they were safe in Judah—or so they thought. Clearly, they worshiped whatever god they concluded could help them the most, little realizing that only one God exists and that this God is the living God of the Scriptures. Their statements condemned them.

God's Final Word on the Faithless People (44:20–30)

One last time the prophet explained that their idolatry had been and remained the reason God was punishing them. Egypt's Pharaoh would be taken prisoner as Zedekiah was, and the Jews who trusted in his protection would die by sword, famine, and peril. For over forty years the people had rejected the word of the Lord that had been sent through Jeremiah. To the end the people refused to accept God's kind offer of forgiveness through repentance. Salvation had been spurned, so judgment was just.

God's Exhortation to Baruch (45:1–5)

Jeremiah was largely unsuccessful in gaining converts to his point of view. Indeed, the text mentions only Baruch and Ebed-Melech as

Baruch, whose name means "blessed," served Jeremiah as an amanuensis or scribe. He appears, moreover, to have had a close personal association with the prophet and to have exercised a significant influence in the ministry of Jeremiah. He wrote down Jeremiah's preaching and read it to the king's counselors who took it to the king. Jehoiakim burned it, but Jeremiah dictated it again (Jer. 36). Jeremiah was even accused of being a mere instrument of Baruch's enmity (Jer. 43:3). The prophet counseled Baruch to place his confidence wholly in the Lord and not to seek great things for himself (Jer. 45). A wide range of later literature was attributed to Baruch in Jewish tradition.

individuals who followed the prophet's lead in preparing for exile. Baruch had especially given himself to Jeremiah's work. He read the prophet's sermon in chapter 36 and suffered alongside his friend. It is understandable, then, that he felt a bit discouraged at how things had turned out in his life. He had been faithful, yet he suffered greatly. Why had God allowed him to endure so much?

God's response, given through Jeremiah, is a telling insight into God's viewpoint on Jerusalem's downfall. God stated that Baruch mourns the loss of great things for himself, but he should not do so. After all, God must tear down all that He built in Israel's history. If anyone had suffered loss, it was the Lord. Even though the punishment had been deserved, it had given God no pleasure in dispensing it. What did please God was granting Baruch his life. Baruch must not seek great things for himself, but he could be sure that the Lord would allow him to live. He would protect him as He had protected Jeremiah. Baruch must see it as a privilege to have served the Lord under difficult circumstances.

- *Idolatry always brings divine punishment.*
- *Meting out punishment gives God no plea-*
- *sure, but God is willing to judge. God's ser-*
- *vants must be satisfied with the role God*
- *gives them.*

GOD'S DISPLEASURE WITH THE NATIONS (46:1–51:64)

Because the Lord is the Creator of the heavens and earth, he has jurisdiction over all nations. Israel was the nation chosen to share God's glory with the rest of the world (Exod. 19:5, 6), but that did not mean God was not concerned about all the rest of the countries and peoples. God loves every person, regardless of race.

GOD WILL JUDGE EGYPT (46:1–28)

Throughout Israelite history, Egypt proved to be an unstable ally for the chosen people. Time after time Egypt promised to help, only to let Israel or Judah face their enemies alone. During Jeremiah's time, Egypt inserted itself into Judah's political system after Pharaoh Neco's army killed Josiah in 609 B.C. (2 Kings 23:28–30). Therefore, over time the Egyptians proved to be both poor ally and destructive enemy, so God had plans for their future.

God Will put Egypt to Shame (46:1–12)

This prophecy about Egypt came to Jeremiah in Jehoiakim's fifth year, or about 605 B.C. During that year, Babylon finally defeated the remnants of Assyria's armies and put Egypt to flight as well. This passage makes it clear that the Lord was using Babylon to punish countries that had been cruel to Judah, not just to chastise Judah. God works in history on behalf of His chosen people, and also works against sinners everywhere.

When Egypt meets Babylon in battle, the Egyptian forces would become terrified and would flee. No matter how hard the Egyptians tried, they would be routed by the superior Babylonian army. It must be understood, however, that this defeat was not some simple historical matter. God was being avenged for Egypt's sins. This battle was the Lord's, and the Lord would win it.

Earlier biblical accounts such as the Hagar stories make this point (Gen. 16:9–16), as do later books such as Jonah. But this concern has another side. The God who sends missionaries to the ends of the earth will also judge the nations for their sins. This section of Jeremiah makes this point by emphasizing the coming judgment on Egypt, Israel's smaller neighbors, and Babylon. Whether great or small, the Lord rules them all.

God Will Judge Egypt's Gods and Kings (46:13–26)

Babylon's victory over Egypt would cause the Egyptians to experience the same sort of oppression they inflicted upon Judah. Once Egypt's armies had fled, the people would suffer loss of property and loss of land. There would be many Egyptian refugees. They would be plundered, and they would lose their political autonomy. Jeremiah made it plain that these events would occur so Egypt's gods would be seen for what they were—nothing. A loving God must punish idolatry, since idolatry cuts off people from their only source of salvation. Likewise, this judgment would expose Egypt's leaders for what they were—pompous blowhards. Egypt's Pharaoh was a hollow man serving nonexistent deities.

God Is with Israel (46:27, 28)

God's people need to know that the Lord is with them, no matter how chaotic world events become. Israel would return to their land, just as Jeremiah 30–33 had promised. They would be corrected for their sins, but the Lord is not finished with them. In the future they will dwell securely in their homes, gratefully serving the Lord.

- *Egypt was an old and great nation, but they*
- *were accountable to God. Because He is kind,*
- *God will judge any nation that practices*
- *idolatry. Israel will be punished, yet will be*
- *renewed in the Lord's timing.*

GOD WILL PUNISH PHILISTIA (47:1–7)

Philistia was one of Israel's most ancient enemies. Starting with the era of the judges (about 1400–1050 B.C.), the Philistines provided determined opposition to Israel's plans. Philistia attempted to remain neutral in the midst of the many regional conflicts of this era, but they were still invaded and defeated by Egypt and Babylon. Jeremiah stated that Egypt's victory over Philistia was God's judgment. It was not merely the result of political or military superiority.

Philistia's major cities—Ekron, Gath, Gaza, and Ashkelon—were on the west coast of Palestine near the Mediterranean Sea.

God Will Destroy the Philistines (47:1–4)

The Scriptures teach that world events do not just happen. The Lord rules and shapes history. Here Jeremiah asserted that a great judgment was coming upon the Philistines. Egypt would be the nation that defeated them, but it was the Lord who sent the Egyptians. The Egyptian invasion would be like a great body of water that rises inexorably above a city, and it would separate Philistia from all allies. No hope for rescue existed.

God's Sword Cannot Be Stilled (47:5–7)

Philistia's punishment seems so devastating that an unidentified voice asked how long it must continue. The answer was that the Lord's punishing sword cannot be silenced, for the Lord has given it an order. In other words, God's judging word cannot be silenced until it has been completely fulfilled. God's wrath is as thorough as God's mercy.

■ *God's judgment is overwhelming and certain*
■ *to fulfill its purpose. Once begun, it will not*
■ *cease until it has chastised the wicked com-*
■ *pletely.*

GOD WILL PUNISH MOAB (48:1–47)

Israel's relationship with Moab went back even
farther than the one with Philistia. Moab's origins dated back to Abraham's era (about 2000
B.C.). At that time the Lord determined to
destroy Sodom and Gomorrah, but He waited
until Lot, Abraham's nephew, could flee from
Sodom (Gen. 19:1–29). Believing that they
would never get married, Lot's daughters got
their father drunk and slept with him. Moab
and Ammon were the two children who
resulted from those incestuous unions (Gen.
19:30–38). The descendants of Moab feared
Israel in Moses' era (about 1450–1400 B.C.), so
they attempted to hire Balaam to curse Israel
(Num. 22:1–7). In virtually every succeeding
era the Moabites and Israelites fought one
another. Thus, Isaiah 15, 16, Ezekiel 25:8–11,
Amos 2:1–3, and Zephaniah 2:8–11 announce
God's coming destruction of Moab. Zephaniah
indicated that Moab's arrogance led to this punishment. Jeremiah agreed, and added that the
Lord will judge Moab because of their commitment to Chemosh, their national deity, who,
like other idols, does not exist.

God Will Punish Moab's Arrogance and Idolatry (48:1–10)

There can be no doubt that Moab will endure
the same type of destruction as the other
nations in the region. Their armies will be over-
powered and their little ones taken captive.

They have arrogantly trusted in their achievements, but they cannot save themselves now (48:7). They have trusted in their god, but Chemosh cannot deliver them, since he does not exist (48:7). Idolatry is the ultimate in human arrogance, for it places the works of human hands above the living God, who created the heavens and the earth.

Chemosh, meaning *subdue*, was a deity the Moabites worshiped (Num. 21:29). He was expected to provide land for Moab (Judg. 11:24). Solomon erected a sanctuary for Chemosh on a mountain east of Jerusalem (1 Kings 11:7).

Moab Will Be Ashamed of Chemosh (48:11–20)

Moab will learn the same lesson as Israel. Just as Israel became ashamed of their empty worship rites practiced at Bethel, so Moab will be ashamed of worshiping Chemosh (48:13). False gods cannot deliver from foreign armies. Only the living God can do so.

Moab's Boasts Will Be Silenced (48:21–44)

This passage reemphasizes Moab's enormous pride. The nation had boasted against the Lord because they had been arrogant toward Israel (48:26–27). No doubt the Moabites had the typical ancient attitude that a deity's power was demonstrated by the might of the people who worshiped that god. Thus, they did not think the Lord was very significant because they saw Israel's weakness. Speaking against Israel and speaking against the Lord became the same thing.

God made it clear that such thinking is unsound and dangerous. If such theology was not changed, then the Lord would punish those who held these views. God does not enjoy judging, but is willing to do so in order to wipe out the terrible effects of idolatry (48:36–44). A loving God cannot allow people to believe lies.

God Will Restore Moab (48:45–47)

Despite all that had been said, the Lord would not make a complete end of Moab. Once the nation has been punished, the people scattered, and love for Chemosh obliterated, the Lord will restore Moab. The specific details of this restoration are not offered, but renewal will occur. God's love is not confined to Israel. The Creator continues to work with persons from all nations and races. God's mercy is global in its scope.

- *God must judge arrogance, for it separates*
- *sinful persons from a loving God. All idola-*
- *try is dangerous to human beings. God must*
- *not be underestimated because of the weak-*
- *nesses of those who worship Him.*

GOD WILL JUDGE AMMON (49:1–6)

Like Moab, Ammon's origins dated back to Lot's daughters' seduction of their father (Gen. 19:30–38).

As was the case with the Moabites, the Ammonites were an old and determined foe of Israel. The Ammonites worshiped Milchom, a god which Solomon introduced to Jerusalem (1 Kings 11:5). As enemies of Israel and as worshipers of a so-called god other than the living God, the Ammonites were candidates for judgment.

Ammon Has Dispossessed Israel (49:1)

God gave each Israelite tribe a specific area of Canaan at the time of the conquest (Josh. 15–19). By Jeremiah's time, the Ammonites possessed part of what had been allotted to the tribe of Gad. Not only did they possess part of the Promised Land; they also worshiped an idol there. Thus, the Lord had decided to remove the Ammonites from their land. The living God would dispossess them and their false god.

Ammon's Boasting Will Cease (49:2–5)

Like Moab and Egypt, Ammon had grown boastful. The Ammonites had also become materialistic (49:4). They trusted in their wealth and security. Their misguided faith would lead to their downfall. God would send terror into their midst, most likely in the form of a Babylonian invasion.

God Will Restore Ammon in the Future (49:6)

As was true of Moab (48:47), the Lord would restore Ammon some time in the future. Judgment was not God's final word for them. Mercy would once again grace their national life.

- God demands sole allegiance from all
- nations. Any arrogant, materialistic nation
- is in danger of divine wrath. God restores the
- fortunes of those who have been punished.

GOD WILL PUNISH EDOM (49:7–22)

Edom's national roots extended back to Esau, Jacob's twin brother (Gen. 36:9–43). Thus, the Edomites were even closer relatives to Israel than the Moabites and Ammonites. As was true of the Philistines, Moabites, and Ammonites, the Edomites had a long history of opposing Israel. As was the case with the Moabites and Ammonites, the Lord's displeasure with Edom did not stem simply from their opposition to Israel. Rather, the problem was that Edom had arrogantly worshiped other gods.

The most scathing statement of Edom's hatred of Israel appears in the book of Obadiah, where the Lord chastises Edom for rejoicing in Jerusalem's downfall and killing refugees from the city.

Edom Has Been Foolish (49:7–11)

Edom prided itself in its tradition of wisdom writing and thinking. They thought that no one could out think or out maneuver them. God stated that their wisdom was not enough to protect them from approaching devastation. Worshiping an idol is the most foolish thing a person can do, and Edom had been guilty of idolatry.

Edom's Arrogance Has Deceived Them (49:12–16)

Edom's cities were built into rock formations. Therefore, it was exceedingly difficult to conquer these strongholds. This security led them to believe that they were safe no matter what world events held, which in turn led them to become arrogant. The Lord stated that Babylon would conquer Edom. In fact, Babylon's task would be made easier by Edom's pride.

God's Purposes for Edom Will Be Fulfilled (49:17–22)

Everything that Jeremiah had said about Edom became part of God's immovable plan for Edom. They would endure punishment. Their cities would be uninhabited. Their people would be exiled. Other nations would be appalled at what they endured. No amount of Edomite bravado would change these realities. God is sovereign over history.

- Arrogance is never an attitude to bring into
- God's presence. God's will is going to occur.
- Arrogance leads to spiritual blindness.

GOD WILL PUNISH DAMASCUS (49:23–27)

Having denounced Judah's southern and eastern neighbors, Jeremiah now turned his attention to the north. His first target was Syria, a country that threatened Israel's security from the ninth century B.C. onward. The once-proud

Syrian nation had become like the rest of the region's smaller countries—helpless before the Babylonian onslaught. Jeremiah promised that gloom, anxiety, distress, and panic would grip Damascus as the enemy overran the city.

■ *Judgment paralyzes a nation through dread*
■ *and depression.*

GOD WILL PUNISH TRIBES NORTH OF SYRIA (49:28–33)

Although it is difficult to determine with certainty what places these verses discuss, it is possible that the prophet targeted tribes north of Syria. If so, Jeremiah's sermons against the nations included lands as far south as Egypt and as far north as beyond Damascus. In other words, God's judgment spans the known world. No place is safe from the Lord's justifiable wrath.

The peoples depicted here were at ease. They had great facility in trading and general commerce. Sadly, their peaceful existence would cease. Those living in rural areas will be judged just as surely as those dwelling in cities.

■ *No one is safe from God's judgment.*

GOD WILL JUDGE THE ENDS OF THE EARTH (49:34–39)

It is hard to determine Elam's exact location. Although there are many suggestions on this matter, it is possible that Jeremiah simply meant that the Lord would judge the ends of the earth.

There is no nation that can sin against the Lord and avoid divine wrath. Neither geographical location nor national heritage insulates one from responsibility to the Creator.

■ *God is no respecter of persons.*

GOD WILL JUDGE BABYLON (50:1–51:64)

Babylon ruled the ancient world from about 609–539 B.C. For years the Babylonians opposed the dominant Assyrians, but they were unable to defeat them until 612 B.C. They proceeded to rout the Egyptians in 609 B.C., and then dominated the fertile crescent. Of course, the Babylonians dominated Judah from 609 B.C. onwards, and they eventually destroyed Jerusalem in 587 B.C. In 539 B.C. the Persians led by Cyrus the Great conquered Babylon and took over its kingdom.

So far, Jeremiah has emphasized Babylon's role as the Lord's instrument of judgment. Time after time the prophet has stated that Babylon's armies will run roughshod over sinful nations. Now, however, it is Babylon that is condemned. The instrument of judgment has become as arrogant as the countries they have defeated, so the Lord must punish them.

These chapters are extraordinary in that they predicted Babylon's fall decades before the disaster occurred. They demonstrate that all nations—great or small—are under the Lord's command. Mighty Babylon, no less than puny Judah, is under the authority of the Creator.

Babylon and Their Gods Will Be Destroyed (50:1–10)

Just as the gods of Egypt, Moab, Edom, and Ammon have been denounced, so the Lord asserts that Babylon's gods will be destroyed. These so-called deities are mere images, and are therefore, no match for the living God. A powerful army will come and defeat Babylon. God will ensure this eventuality.

When Babylon is defeated, the chosen people will be gathered and returned to their land. This promise came true in 538 B.C., when Cyrus allowed the Jews to go back to Jerusalem. Exile was never God's final plan for Israel, as Jeremiah 30–33 has already made plain.

Babylon Has Sinned against the Lord (50:11–16)

Babylon has sinned against the Lord by acting as if their many victories are the result of their own power. The Lord has given them the other nations, but Babylon has arrogantly assumed that they have done everything on their own. By now Jeremiah has made it clear how God views such attitudes.

God Will Gather and Pardon Israel (50:17–20)

In due time, Israel will return to the Promised Land. At that time a remnant will possess their ancestral home. This remnant will be forgiven. Their sins will be forgotten, and the people will have a fresh start with the Lord.

Babylon Will Be Judged Like Sodom and Gomorrah (50:21–40)

Babylon will be so utterly destroyed that only wild animals will live there. This devastation will occur because Babylon has fought against the Lord (50:24), has been arrogant against the Lord (50:29), and has loved many idols (50:38). God will gain vengeance for the destruction of the Temple (50:28) by making Babylon as desolate as Sodom and Gomorrah. From the greatest to the least, all the Babylonians will feel the sting of God's wrath.

God's Purposes Will Be Fulfilled (50:41–46)

These plans for judgment cannot be thwarted, and they will not be repealed. God has determined the time for Babylon's punishment. No one can successfully dispute God's right to do what Jeremiah has described.

Israel's history during the 150 years prior to the writing of this passage was rather dismal. Assyria conquered the ten northern tribes in 722 B.C., then Babylon destroyed the southern two tribes in 587 B.C. The chosen people had endured horrible atrocities. Still, the Lord judged Assyria through Babylon, and in due time God would judge the Babylonians by sending the Persians against them. Thus, the Jews must understand that God is still keeping ancient promises made to Abraham and David.

God Has Not Forsaken Israel (51:1–10)

All that had been said about Israel's eventual renewal did not change the fact that the Jews sinned against the Lord by breaking the Mosaic Covenant. Israel has merited punishment. Yet the Lord still loved Israel, and still had plans to bless the chosen ones. God would vindicate Israel by setting them free from the Babylonians. God would be as active on their behalf as He was for their destruction.

God the Creator Will Shatter Babylon (51:11–23)

One of the Bible's strongest arguments against idolatry is the fact that the Lord made the heavens and the earth. If God alone and God working alone made the world, then idols have no claim on human beings. If the idols had no part in making the world, then they are not real. They have no God-ness.

"Now the LORD had said unto Abram, Get thee out of thy country, and from thy kindred, and from thy father's house, unto a land that I will shew thee:
And I will make of thee a great nation, and I will bless thee, and make thy name great; and thou shalt be a blessing:
And I will bless them that bless thee, and curse him that curseth thee: and in thee shall all families of the earth be blessed."
(Gen. 12:1–3, KJV).

Individuals who worship idols are therefore venerating the works of their hands. Idols have no breath, no life, no validity. They simply weary those who serve them, so they are worthless.

God Will Destroy Babylon for Israel's Sake (51:24–58)

God will judge Babylon for what they did to Jerusalem. All the violence done to the Jews will come back on the Babylonians' heads. God Himself will plead Jerusalem's case against their tormenters (51:34–36). Babylon will be reduced to rubble, just as Jerusalem had been. Indeed, all those oppressed by Babylon will be avenged when the great city becomes a vast wasteland. Babylon may stockpile weapons to the sky, but they can be certain that God will guarantee their demise (51:52–53).

God Will Cause Babylon to Sink Like a Rock (51:59–64)

One more time the Lord called upon Jeremiah to do a symbolic act. He instructed a man named Seraiah to take the scroll of these prophecies, tie a rock to them, and throw them in the Euphrates River. This act symbolized the inevitable sinking of Babylon as a nation. Again, it is amazing that these predictions were offered years before they actually came to pass. Only a divine Word could be true in such detail.

■ *All nations are under God's control. The*
■ *Lord never ceases to work on behalf of His*
■ *people. Arrogance and idolatry can destroy*
■ *even a mighty nation. God's word always*
■ *comes true.*

CONCLUSION (52:1–34)

The prophecy ends with a lengthy description of the fall of Jerusalem and the fate of Jehoiachin, the king exiled in 597 B.C. This material is found nearly word for word in 2 Kings 24:18–25:30, which shows the importance of these events in Israelite history. No greater loss ever befell the nation in Old Testament times. Not until a similar defeat occurred at the hands of the Romans in A.D. 70 did the Jews suffer such a calamity. The destruction of Jerusalem vindicated all that the Lord had threatened. Jeremiah's predictions did come to pass.

THE FALL OF JERUSALEM AND ZEDEKIAH'S BLINDING (52:1–11)

Much of what is recounted here was already depicted in Jeremiah 39:1–18. In a matter-of-fact way, the author states that the Babylonian siege resulted in the city's fall. As the capital was about to be entered, the king and his court attempted to flee, but they were captured by their enemies. Zedekiah was forced to watch his sons executed, then had his eyes put out. His spiritual blindness had led to actual blindness. His poor leadership had taken his country to defeat. Now the Jews were bereft of the city that they believed was special to the Lord.

THE BABYLONIANS DESTROY THE TEMPLE (52:12–3)

When Solomon built the Temple, the Lord promised to place His name there as long as the people served Him (1 Kings 9:1–9). The nation had not kept their end of the covenant, so the Lord was justified in judging now. The place where forgiveness was secured, praise was offered, and instruction was given lay in ruins. Priests and people no longer had access to the place that gave them a feeling of security. Many Jews probably wondered if God still cared for them.

THE PEOPLE ARE SENT INTO EXILE (52:24–30)

Israel had lost its king, its capital, and its Temple. Now it would lose its people. Babylon sent the most useful of the population to distant lands to join those who were taken captive in 605 and 597 B.C. Only the poorest and least skilled persons were allowed to remain, and as Jeremiah 42–44 had already stated, these individuals did not obey the Babylonians. They foolishly opposed the governor put in place by the conquerors. Israel would stay in exile until Cyrus allowed them to return in 538 B.C.

GOD HAS NOT FORSAKEN DAVID'S DESCENDANTS (52:31–34)

Jeremiah ends with a small bit of hope. Exiled for thirty-seven years, Jehoiachin was given preferential treatment in his declining years. This conclusion demonstrates that God's eternal covenant with David continued in effect. As long as the Davidic lineage continued, the promise of the king mentioned in Jeremiah 23:1–8 remained alive. Israel may sink into decline, defeat, and exile, yet the Lord is not finished with the chosen people. As Jeremiah 30–33 makes plain, there is still a future hope for the people of God.

Jeremiah's message is relevant today. Nations continue to act arrogantly toward God and toward one another. Even those committed to the Lord sometimes sin and refuse to repent. Our world's only hope is to seek the living God of the Scriptures and to be part of the remnant that relates to the Lord through the New Covenant. Christians believe that Jesus is the Savior promised in Jeremiah 23:1–8 and that the New Covenant was begun through Christ's blood. All who would flee the coming judgment must repent, trust the Savior, be part of the remnant, teach the Scriptures, live justly, and share God's grace with others. If we do so, then Jeremiah's ministry will not be in vain. Indeed, it will continue to bear fruit.

- *God's promise to judge will be fulfilled if per-*
- *sons and nations fail to repent. God's judg-*
- *ment has personal and community*
- *ramifications. God's promises to heal must*
- *be realized.*

QUESTIONS TO GUIDE YOUR STUDY

1. List three major judgments against Israel.
2. How did Jehoiakim react to God's Word on the scroll?
3. What was Babylon's policy toward those left in Judah when Gedaliah was governor? How was this policy received?
4. Where did Jeremiah go into exile?

LAMENTATIONS

Lamentations, a book composed of five chapters, follows Jeremiah in our English Bibles. In the Hebrew Bible it is contained in the third section—the Writings.

HISTORICAL SETTING

Lamentations expresses the profound grief experienced by God's people upon the destruction of Jerusalem. It is difficult to overestimate the shock and sorrow which followed the series of events which brought Jerusalem down.

God had promised and given the land to Abraham and his heirs. It was now taken away. The Temple, the place where God dwelled in the midst of His people, was destroyed.

Where was God? Did God's people have a future?

Tradition has linked Lamentations to Jeremiah, partly because of 2 Chronicles 35:25, which says he issued a lamentation for Josiah.

AUTHOR, DATE, AND AUDIENCE

Lamentations was almost certainly written after Jerusalem's destruction in 587 B.C.

Like Psalm 119, it employs acrostic poetry. In chapters 1, 2, and 4, each succeeding verse begins with the next letter of the Hebrew alphabet. Chapter 3 has three such poems.

JERUSALEM'S SORROW (1:1–22)

Jerusalem is likened to a grieving widow. She was once a queen. Now she is a slave. Once surrounded by friends, she is now alone with none to comfort her.

The roads to Jerusalem likewise take on human features: They mourn. Once they brought joyful pilgrims to Jerusalem. Now they are desolate.

Jerusalem recognizes that her suffering is no accident. The Lord has brought this on her. She recognizes that her sin and uncleanness have been the occasion for this destruction.

GOD'S JUSTIFIABLE WRATH (2:1–22)

God has poured out tremendous destruction on Israel. This punishment reverses past blessings. Now instead of leading Israel with a pillar of cloud, He covers them "with a cloud of his anger." Once God fought for Israel, but He has now become their enemy (vv. 2–5). He appointed the tabernacle and altar as special places once, but now the Lord has rejected them both (vv. 6–7). Zion was a favored city, but no more.

During the Exodus, "By day the Lord went ahead of them in a pillar of cloud to guide them on their way and by night in a pillar of fire to give them light, so that they could travel by day or night" (Exod. 13:21).

Israel brought God's wrath on themselves. They listened to false prophets (v. 14) and ran after idols. All the people can do now is to ask God to save them (vv. 20–22).

A GLIMMER OF HOPE (3:1–66)

The narrator now changes. He is "a man who has seen affliction." In spite of God's wrath directed at His people and their city, the narrator dares to hope. With the destruction evident everywhere, the prophet knows that God's mercy is greater than His wrath. God is faithful. His mercies are new every morning. God prefers mercy to wrath, but the continued responses of His people left Him no alternative but to destroy Jerusalem.

The narrator has the maturity to say that we, God's people, brought this on ourselves. He calls on the survivors to cease complaining, to search their hearts, to confess their sins, and to return to God. This afflicted one will persist in his intercession to God for mercy. He calls on

God to punish those whom God has used as the instruments of wrath against Jerusalem.

GOD'S ANGER FULLY SPENT (4:1–22)

Chapter 4 continues a detailed description of the state of Jerusalem. Circumstances are difficult. Children are ill-treated and even ignored by their parents. Some mothers have resorted to cannibalism. The wealthy who once enjoyed the finest fare are looking for scraps—anything to keep body and soul together. Jerusalem has reached the depths of despair. God's anger has been fully poured out on His people.

A PLEA FOR RESTORATION (5:1–22)

Contrasts continue between the former glory of Jerusalem and her people and the present desolation of the city. Once again the prophet recognizes that sin has brought about this disaster. Still, the prophet confesses that God reigns from generation to generation. He asks why God must forsake His people for so long and calls on Him to restore His people.

QUESTIONS TO GUIDE YOUR STUDY

1. What is an acrostic poem?
2. What event does Lamentations mourn?
3. What attitude does "the man of affliction" take regarding what has happened to Jerusalem?
4. In the midst of mourning for Jerusalem, what glimmer of hope is seen and what is the basis for this hope?

The following is a collection of Broadman & Holman published reference sources used for this work. They are provided here to meet the reader's need for more specific information and/or for an expanded treatment of the books of Jeremiah and Lamentations. All of these works will greatly aid the reader's study, teaching, and presentation of the books of Jeremiah and Lamentations. The accompanying annotations can be helpful in guiding the reader to the proper resources.

Cate, Robert L. *An Introduction to the Old Testament and Its Study*. An introductory work presenting background information, issues related to interpretation, and summaries of each book of the Old Testament.

Dalglish, Edward R., *Jeremiah, Lamentations* (Laymen's Bible Book Commentary, vol. 11). A concise commentary on Jeremiah and Lamentations.

Dockery, David S., Kenneth A. Mathews, and Robert B. Sloan. *Foundations for Biblical Interpretation: A Complete Library of Tools and Resources*. A comprehensive introduction to matters relating to the composition and interpretation of the entire Bible. This work includes a discussion of the geographical, historical, cultural, religious, and political backgrounds of the Bible.

Farris, T. V. *Mighty to Save: A Study in Old Testament Soteriology*. A wonderful evaluation of many Old Testament passages that teach about salvation. This work makes a conscious attempt to apply Old Testament teachings to the Christian life.

Francisco, Clyde T. *Introducing the Old Testament*. Revised edition. An introductory guide to each of the books of the Old Testament. This work includes a discussion on how to interpret the Old Testament.

Holman Bible Dictionary. An exhaustive, alphabetically arranged resource of Bible-related subjects. An excellent tool of definitions and other information on people, places, things, and events of the books Jeremiah and Lamentations.

Holman Bible Handbook. A summary treatment of each book of the Bible that offers outlines, commentary on key themes and sections, illustrations, charts, maps, and full-color photos. This tool also provides an accent on broader theological teachings of the Bible.

Holman Book of Biblical Charts, Maps, and Reconstructions. This easy-to-use work provides numerous color charts on various matters related to Bible content and background, maps of important events, and drawings of objects, buildings, and cities mentioned in the Bible.

Huey, F. B., Jr. *Jeremiah, Lamentations* (The New American Commentary, vol. 16). A scholarly treatment that emphasizes the text of Jeremiah and Lamentations, its backgrounds, theological considerations, issues in interpretation, and summaries of scholarly debates on important points.

Sandy, D. Brent and Ronald L. Giese, Jr. *Cracking Old Testament Codes: A Guide to Interpreting the Literary Genres of the Old Testament.* This book is designed to make scholarly discussions available to preachers and teachers.

Smith, Ralph L. *Old Testament Theology: Its History, Method, and Message.* A comprehensive treatment of various issues relating to Old Testament theology. Written for university and seminary students, ministers, and advanced lay teachers.

SHEPHERD'S NOTES

SHEPHERD'S NOTES

SHEPHERD'S NOTES

SHEPHERD'S
NOTES